Praise for *Inner*

'*Inner Spark* is a book that will help you move through difficult times, and remind you of your own greatness.'

Deepak Chopra, MD, author of *Metahuman: Unleashing Your Infinite Potential*

'Kristin Vikjord's book bursts from the mind of a psychologist and the soul of a powerful teacher, as deep as the Nordic waters. Kristin has a unique, healing, and important voice. I highly recommend it.'

Max Strom, speaker, breathing teacher, and author of *A Life Worth Breathing* and *There is No App for Happiness*

'Kristin Vikjord has a very readable, relatable and lively writing style. The reader is skillfully guided how to re-ignite their "Inner Spark" through easy to adopt changes and techniques.'

Shirley Telles MBBS, MPhil, PhD (Neurophysiology), DSc (Yoga), Director, Patanjali Research Foundation, Haridwar, India

'Kristin elegantly weaves contemporary psychology with essential teachings of mindfulness, into a beautiful and practical guidance book. Kristin is a leading voice in contemporary spirituality.'

Lea Loncar MSc (Psychology), Founder of Zenit Yoga and Samvid Yoga, NTNU University of Trondheim Lecturer

'Chock full of practical wisdom that can help us not only survive, but to flourish during difficult times.'

Ronald D. Siegel, Psy.D., Assistant Professor of
Psychology, Harvard Medical School,
and author of *The Mindfulness Solution:
Everyday Practices for Everyday Problems*

'Down to earth, and heart opening, this book full of personal stories and practical methods will revive that flickering spark within you. A precious gem to carry with you always.'

Lama Tsultrim Allione, author of
*Wisdom Rising: Journey into the Mandala
of the Empowered Feminine*

'Kristin Vikjord's book is here to help you intelligently reveal your own inner spark and experience more luminosity in every area of your life.'

Elena Brower, author
of *Practice You, A Journal*

'This book makes the radical but liberating suggestion that cultivating psychological health might be less a war we need to wage with ourselves, in this case to make suffering stop, and more about making peace with our embodied experience right now as it is.'

David Emerson YACEP, TCTSY-F, Director
The Center for Trauma and Embodiment at JRI, author
of *Trauma-Sensitive Yoga in Therapy* and co-author of
Overcoming Trauma Through Yoga

Inner Spark

KRISTIN VIKJORD

Inner Spark

Finding Calm in
a Stressful World

bluebird
books for life

First published 2019 by Kosmos Uitgevers

First published in the UK 2020 by Bluebird
an imprint of Pan Macmillan
The Smithson, 6 Briset Street, London EC1M 5NR
Associated companies throughout the world
www.panmacmillan.com

ISBN 978-1-5290-4359-4 TPB

9 8 7 6 5 4 3 2 1

A CIP catalogue record for this book is available from the British Library.

Typeset by Palimpsest Book Production Ltd, Falkirk, Stirlingshire
Printed and bound by CPI Group (UK) Ltd, Croydon, CR0 4YY

Visit **www.panmacmillan.com** to read more about all our books
and to buy them. You will also find features, author interviews and
news of any author events, and you can sign up for e-newsletters
so that you're always first to hear about our new releases.

Contents

Disclaimer

This book is an invitation to contemplation and movement to agency in the reader. The programme in its whole is meant as support, an inspiration and nudge to action more than anything else. The aim is to empower readers to take action, and to increase their knowledge and connect the dots to access and draw on their own wisdom, to step out of their emotional struggle and the feeling of being stuck. All patient stories are fictional but inspired by therapeutic themes from the author's work and life. The rationale and contraindications for the recommended practices in the Wellbeing Prescriptions are presented; however, they are not to be considered as treatment for mental health disease and disorders. They are offered as hope in one's journey of emotional transitions. As you read, take what resonates with you and leave the rest behind.

'In the search for everything, I found that there was nothing, and I could rest with ease in the ebb and flow of unease.'

To my grandmothers, my mother, and sisters. To my dearest friends, and soul dancers, and to my teachers. To all the women carrying the past and the future on their hips, in their arms, in their comforting words, in their experience of difficulty.

To my father, for showing that life is much more than work. To my husband, for continuously igniting my Spark. For continuously reminding me of the greatness of it all, beyond anything imaginable. To my sons, for being so sparkly and alive with roaring, jumping laughter. For teaching me heartfulness, and living life from Inner Spark.

Author's Note

This book and its contents were written well before the Covid-19 pandemic and the subsequent societal lockdowns. The impact of prolonged social isolation on any individual may differ broadly, but, for many, it affects the maintenance of general health, especially mental health. As a strenuous exercise for most people, the lockdown intensified difficulties for those already struggling psychologically or going through hardships.

The exercises throughout this book are well suited for the stresses and challenges we have all experienced as a result of the lockdown. Following the course of this book, you'll find practices that offer relief and support in unravelling the psychological implications of social isolation. The Wellbeing Prescriptions are curated in a manner that will benefit you in any psychological challenge or intense emotional situation, and the Readiness for Change tools are a valuable map to guide you through those struggles, leading you to the right actions for you.

I invite you to use this book as your support and encourage you to dive into it to reach your resilience. Even though we may find ourselves in challenges that seem complicated or overwhelming, there's always a way to move through. A way held in compassion, in understanding, rather than a way that is destructive and harmful. This book provides you with tools and simple action points that will lessen feelings of overwhelm and help guide you, steadfastly and tenderly, out of stress. They will provide you with the understanding required to find a path back to your strength and Inner Spark.

Stay gentle and be patient. Goodness is on the horizon.

With warmest regards,
Kristin

Inner Spark

Introduction

I was named after my father's mother, Kirstin. She lived at the foot of majestic mountains illuminated by the midnight sun and cornered by the wild, icy ocean of the Lofoten Islands. She lived through many hardships as a girl and was a mother of six children. In addition to taking care of her large family, which included her in-laws, she also took care of the family's livestock and farmland in order to feed everyone. She passed away not far from where I am sitting right now, at the top of a hill with a view of the town, the mountains and the fjord.

I knew her as a warm, bosomy grandmother who always had home-made dishes ready for visiting family. She smelled of roses, wore pale pink nail polish and flowery dresses, and had a head topped with curly hair. My father's childhood memories painted stories for me of a life he adored and they only added to my love for her. But when I was older he began sharing other stories: of a mother with a temper who sometimes spoke harshly to his older siblings, or of the slap of her hand on her children's soft cheeks. This was a side of her that was foreign to me. Oddly, hearing these stories when I was an adult made me appreciate her all the more fully. The picture I had of her, and that I had held in my mind for so long, actually came to life as I realized her hardships and attempts to cope with them. My fairy grandmother became real.

In my early twenties she said to me: 'You have a spark, Kristin. Bubbly like a glass of champagne.' I took her sweet words as a compliment, but they didn't really stick with me. Then a decade later I became a mother for the first time. Motherhood brought me not only the obvious and expected changes: changes for my body, in how I spent my time and what I focused on daily. I also found myself in an all-enveloping wave of existential self-inquiry. Becoming a mother unexpectedly became a major turning point in my life at deep levels I had not been prepared for; I hadn't realized the biochemical response would have such an impact. The embodiment of my new role as a parent and a mother meant I felt emotional most of the time and like I was constantly on alert. After the arrival of our second son, the daily grind of parenthood, which was by then well into its fourth year of constant broken sleep, started to take its toll. I noticed that I felt like a qualitatively different person. The kind words of my grandmother resurfaced, and this time they resonated with me profoundly. I saw that my Inner Spark had drained out of me. I recognized that my Inner Spark had once been there but now it had disappeared. Maybe you can relate: maybe you once felt more joyous and more alive, more radiant and energized, and now that feeling is just a distant memory.

I knew I had more hardship ahead of me. I knew life wouldn't hit the pause button for me just because that would be convenient. If I was to reclaim my Inner Spark, then I needed to take action. So I did. I started writing passionately. Words started pouring out of me in stories and in bits and pieces. A longing for creativity, spontaneity, and playfulness struck me by surprise, and I continued. Along the way I found my Inner Spark and I reconnected to my sense of self.

I found a way to embrace the struggle of motherhood instead of resisting it.

This book is about how to step out of emotional struggle while you are going through any of the difficult transition periods of life, like new motherhood. First of all, I believe we all have that Inner Spark. I'll let you know exactly what it is later, but for now believe this: Inner Spark is innate. It is an effect of being alive. But it's easy to lose sight of.

We simply don't thrive in discomfort or in unease. We don't thrive when we are stressed. In recent years a multimillion-dollar industry has grown around stress reduction and stress management. It is a well-known fact that over time elevated stress levels are detrimental to our health.

However, not all stress is actually that awful. Almost everything we are exposed to is a stressor and has the potential to activate our inner alarm systems. We are receptive to stress because our brains and nervous systems are wired to alarm us when necessary. Being hungry or thirsty or feeling anxious and lonely are all expressions of this alarm system and are healthy signals for us to take action and ensure our survival. These signals tell us to look for food, find water, seek safety, and stay close to our tribes.

Almost everyone, myself included, wants to be free from struggle. We want ease, happiness, more sun, less sun, we want to play more, be more diligent but not too serious, we want to reach our goals, be stress-free, make more money, have no anxiety, no depression, have muscle tone but not too much, eat healthily, drink less, live life as a party, be in a relationship, keep our sacred space, be this not that, and so on. Welcome to the crazy dance of aversion and desire. Human beings are wired so that they constantly want to move away from struggle and unease. We want things to be different, usually easier. This desire is what drives us, like a motor.

So why, we may wonder, aren't we always changing our lives, if change is what we always want and our systems are wired to respond to stress and move us to act? As a psychologist I've met many people, both women and men, who desperately hold on to difficulty and to the struggles they actually want to liberate themselves from. They hold on as though the struggle is a lifeline. Quite naturally, in doing this they increase their controlling behaviours and can find themselves failing dramatically while trying to control the situation and their own unease. Their critical inner voices then turn the volume up. They judge themselves, their thoughts, their feelings, others, or they compare themselves to strangers, in an attempt to organize the inner chaos, which continues to grow. They want change even more, and they struggle even more. The ride of challenging times will take each of us on very different journeys depending on the conditions we grew up in, the quality of relationships that were examples to us, and our unique biogenetic luggage. So many factors determine how compassionately we are able to meet ourselves in challenging times.

Yet for most of us it is true that, as much as we want change, we also cling to the status quo. We want life to be a joyous dance, but we cannot let go of what has entrapped us even when it causes us harm and negativity. This is largely due to the fact that we thrive under predictable conditions, even when these conditions are unhealthy. We cling to what may not be serving us because what is known is predictable and represents safety. We don't change our thoughts and behaviours, and our emotions then don't transform either. Although we want change, we stay put. We just don't know how to step out of this vicious circle. The complex topic of readiness for change is something we will explore in depth throughout this book.

Understanding readiness for change will help you manifest real change. To actually release yourself from the claws of what is no longer serving you is the goal ahead of us. I'll guide you along this path, sharing the essential steps that need to be taken to move out of emotional struggle and into lasting change. But before we really get started, I want to share here and now the important thing you need if you are truly intent on rediscovering your Inner Spark: you need to commit to being patient. Patient with yourself, with how you think, how you feel. And with the process of change. And you need to be willing to do some serious self-inquiry and to take agency.

My reasons for writing this book are many. First of all, I want to support you in your struggle and help you reclaim your Inner Spark. I am convinced you can. Second, I want to contribute to the global discussion on how to live a good life. I believe that in this day and age the way we lead our lives and the societal contexts of our lives – with all the specific challenges of our time – require us to take care of our emotional wellbeing in an unprecedented way. We deserve a beautiful life. A life with ease, even in times of unease.

I hope this book becomes your home-based retreat where you go to spend time with yourself as your own best friend. A space for you to connect to yourself with kindness and patience and to reconnect to the essence of who you are. A space for you to step away from all the doing, the turmoil and the time-directed tyranny. You'll be guided into inquiring into yourself through practices, exercises, and questions for reflection. We will peel away at the messy layers of your behaviours, thoughts, and emotions, and find at the very core of you your Inner Spark. Here you will discover that your sense of purpose, hope, and meaning are alive and well.

Inner Spark is when you are inhabiting a place of freedom, free from thoughts based in fear, free from controlling behaviours, free from attempting to imprison negative emotions, free from unhealthy habits. Inner Spark is when you can access and cultivate emotional wellbeing. When you can hold space for yourself, your heart (read: emotions), and then go on to more skilfully hold space for others and their emotions.

How this book is structured

Inner Spark is a guide to reviving your playfulness when you feel suffocated due to over-scheduled everyday life, due to the stressful desire to create financial comfort for yourself, and due to the daily maintenance of your wellbeing. With all these needs to meet, the depletion spiral is easy to fall into and you may find yourself caught in a dark web and struggle to free yourself. You feel ready for change, but don't know where to start or how to embark on the next step.

This book gives you the skills you need in such overwhelming times. It helps you clarify what brought you here in the first place and what you wish to see changed. It helps you sort through your own inner unease and gives you Nudges to Action towards more ease and playfulness. Ultimately this book reveals how you can (re-)find your Inner Spark.

The book is structured in three parts. Part I: Normalizing contextualizes the topic of struggling as related to stress, feeling overwhelmed, and dealing with emotional unease. Part II: Clarifying will guide you through the first steps of inquiry in order to clarify and create awareness, and includes

Nudges to Action towards positive change. In this part you will verbalize which parts of your life you wish to be different. You will also discover what's hindering you from moving in that direction. Part III is about taking agency and will help you discover how to step out of struggle and how to walk your path to your Inner Spark. Each chapter ends with an invitation to practise, to reflect, to contemplate, or to inquire into yourself and uncover the conditionings that control your inner landscape. Moving through this book you will find refuge in yourself, connect with your Inner Spark, and learn to embody your greatness.

I have written *Inner Spark* for all of you who are ready to make a change in your life. I have written this as a mother but also as a woman with a career and with dreams and ambitions. It is an ode to all of you looking for change, and to my patients who have trusted me and shown me real courage in each of their journeys. I am immensely grateful for all they have shared. And it is an ode to my grandmother, who showed me that hardship need not stand in the way of a good and happy life.

PART I

Normalizing

This time, now:
From inner dark to
Inner Spark

CHAPTER 1

Inner Dark
Leaning into darkness

I was born under the Aurora Borealis. Under the dancing lights of winter. I grew up in moonlit darkness. In the land of the midnight sun, a land where the sun never sets. Where the moon and the sun shine simultaneously. Where the silence is quieter than the first stillness. And time is present, like moments that never pass. Blue hours of vastness. Raw. Pure. Where heaven meets earth in winds as wild as your wildest dreams.

My path into it all

I grew up in nature and my childhood was simple and enjoyable. I loved making bonfires and playing with Barbie dolls or watching David Attenborough's nature programmes or Disney movies. But most of all I loved lying on the ground outside. It didn't matter to me if I lay myself down in the freezing snow or in the summer grass, between the trees in the woods, or out by the shore of the lake where we spent holidays and weekends. I also loved jumping in the rain puddles outside our red wooden house in Bodø, where my parents still live. We climbed in the trees and made blueberry soup on the bonfire. We walked to each other's houses, knocking on doors to see who wanted to come out and play. We walked to school in winter storms so cold that the wind froze our cheeks and we couldn't move our faces. We laughed when we couldn't move our mouths due to the icy winds. And then we laughed even harder because we looked so ridiculous. My friends and I swore to each other that we'd move to a place of eternal summer when we grew up. And when we were old enough, we moved away, we travelled the world. And then we moved back. Always returning to our land in the north, where the lines between heaven and earth are blurred.

· ·

Did you know ...
that being in nature has a positive effect on emotional wellbeing? Gazing out at the horizon, hanging out on the beach, looking for seashells, hiking – sounds inviting, doesn't it? The effects of nature on mental health have been studied for decades now and an increasing body of research confirms that connectedness and immersion in nature enhance mental health and emotional wellbeing. Doctors are even prescribing exposure to nature as a non-medical intervention to improve physical and mental wellbeing.

· ·

A few years ago during a silent retreat a memory suddenly came to me. I saw my nine-year-old self leaning against the doorway of our kitchen, talking to my sister who is two years my senior. The topic was my upcoming tenth birthday. *The Little Mermaid* was playing on our VHS in the background. My sister announced that soon I would enter my teens, and wouldn't it be cool that we would be teenagers together?

I asked what was cool about that, suspecting a hidden agenda. Jealousy was very much a part of our dynamic at that age. But she meant nothing malicious. She said everyone thought it was cool to be a teenager and I asked her why. 'Because you'll never be a child again,' she said. *What?!* I thought. *Never be a child again? Wasn't life going to stay like this, with* The Little Mermaid *on our TV, in the simplicity and safety of our home, forever?!* I felt shaken right down to the core of my existence, and a deep pain surged inside of me. I felt sadness over something I had no control over, and I was overcome by a sense of loss. The awareness of inevitable change, of impermanence, had taken up residence inside of me.

From then on, I did everything I could think of to slow down or even stop this change from happening. It was as if I believed I could somehow learn to control time, and I began adapting my behaviour in an effort to keep the growing discomfort at bay. I fluctuated between periods of extreme neatness and extreme messiness in an attempt to regain a sense of control. At first this helped me feel like I had power over where I was heading, and it helped me realize my own agency regarding what I wanted to focus on and how I was going to do that. I found that I could choose an activity or behaviour that I could excel in and distract myself from my unease. At least for a while.

By the time I was fifteen I was seriously struggling with my attempts to understand the meaning of life. I was hungry for answers and agonized by questions. I had read *Sophie's World* by the brilliant Jostein Gaarder and made my first acquaintance with philosophy, but I wanted more. Not long after that, I stumbled into existential psychology when I read Irvin D. Yalom's novel *When Nietzsche Wept.* I was deeply intrigued by what I read because I recognized the growing unease within myself as part of something human. In retrospect I understand that this was one of the tougher turning points in my life, as it is for most kids with hormone-ridden teenage brains. The worries manifested as restless sensations in my belly at night. Being drawn between ease and unease caused anxiousness, and I began to become aware of these forces and of the constant stream of thoughts tumbling over each other. My inner dialogue went something like: 'Oh, I wish I had that handbag. My life would be so different then.' Or: 'I'm going to stop doing this or that, and only be super-good at that other thing, and then my whole life will change.' When I was seventeen I read my first book on Indian philosophy and immediately felt the urge to learn more. I set out to read whatever I could find on this subject. I loved reading about the mysticism of Hindu spirituality, and I loved discovering that there were philosophical schools that revolved around questions and struggles of living this embodied human life.

I knew early on that I wanted to study psychology. In my pre-teens the deep feeling of unease born of the realization that change is inevitable transformed itself into a meaningful desire to understand the human psyche. But before starting university, I worked in a nursing home for a year. I figured I needed some hands-on experience in healthcare if I was to become a psychologist. In the nursing home, I found that I could make an impact by the humble act of taking care of old and sick people as they moved towards the end of their lives. The experience connected me to life in a new way as I got to know these people in their final life phase. I had the honour of sitting with some of them as they drew their last breath. The impact was huge and completely changed me.

When I went to university to study psychology a year later, I also began a formal practice of yoga. It was there, on my yoga mat, that I found the missing pieces to the puzzle I had been trying to put together. Practising yoga felt like a long exhale, a sigh of relief. I knew I had found something essential, though I'm not sure I could have told you at the time exactly what I had found. The yoga practice resonated in each layer of my being. Being simultaneously aware of my thoughts, emotions, and body, and letting this be an integrated experience simply through movement and breath was nothing short of magical to me. From there on I found myself moving from a new awareness, a new perspective. Little did I know that this would be the start of many beautiful relationships in my life. Learning yoga took me to India and then to Amsterdam, where one summer night under the rays of the full moon I met my future husband. As our relationship grew, I moved to Amsterdam and established Delight Yoga. The love story began with me teaching a few classes weekly in what was then called Delight Studio, to now providing space for more than a hundred teachers. From a handful of students to now supporting many more students in practising ease, focus, and awareness in busy lives, through multiple platforms online and offline. My husband and I continue to curate platforms and meeting places for people to practise yoga and meditation, and engage in practices that facilitate inner peace for themselves and others.

In addition, as a psychologist I have applied mindfulness and yoga (the latter as moving meditation) in clinical settings and as part of treatment plans for a decade. I have shared my knowledge with patients and colleagues on how to find ease in times of unease. Now, with this book, I'm sharing it with you so that you can understand yourself better by looking into the struggle that is causing the suffering. And so you can develop a different, more beneficial relationship with yourself in times of pain. I'm sharing with you the crossroads where the essences of these practices intersect with psychology; and why moving through inner dark is such an essential part of being human today.

Context is personal

I was born in the literal darkness of midwinter in the north of Norway, where winters are dark for months on end. But there was not only darkness; I grew up in a land where summers are light twenty-four hours a day, seven days a week. This makes for an interesting circadian rhythm. The seasons affect you at this latitude and it is essential that you learn to be aware of your energy levels in relation to your surroundings, and most of all in relation to the presence of light. Work hours are shorter in winter than in summer at these latitudes. And when I was growing up, food platters were seasonal, and traditional cooking reflected our local produce.

I learned early on that as human beings we can expect to be affected by our immediate surroundings, by light or darkness, by mountains or skyscrapers. Similarly we are affected by our inner environment, which also directly affects our health. Reduced sun exposure over time and a lack of magnesium in your diet can both affect your moods. Just as a gene pool of hereditary disorders like anxiety and depression, or growing up with an unpredictable raging or moody parent, can similarly affect our emotional health.

By my definition 'immediate surroundings' includes the

generally accepted attitudes and beliefs of the society in which we reside. We'll explore this in depth in the next chapter, but the executive summary is this: being busy has become a status symbol, and exhaustion symptoms are becoming the norm. In a society where sacrificing your own health is no big deal, it is more difficult than ever to draw a line and communicate when a boundary has been crossed. This is certain to put out your Inner Spark.

Slow living and the secularization of Eastern practices, such as mindfulness or contemporary yoga, have helped bring back the coolness of hitting pause every so often. But it's complicated. The way we thrive and strive to live in contentedness is not only a personal affair; there is a matrix of factors involved that we have very little control over. Thriving is societal, environmental, financial, psychological, physiological, educational, and biological. And we have a long way to go before we really do away with the idea that we can thrive as overworked, exhausted multitaskers in today's fast-paced world.

Inner Spark will show you the many factors that have an impact on you, and which factors you can exercise agency over. With these insights, you will see quite clearly how you can step out of emotional struggle, how you can move through your inner darkness to Inner Spark. When we can actively and consciously draw on resources to increase our emotional wellbeing at the levels of both our inner and outer surroundings, we move with ease towards more integrated health, and thus a beautiful life.

In my work as a psychologist, I work to empower my patients and help them unravel their struggles and willingly and safely access their inner darkness, which is a crucial step towards understanding themselves better. From there it is possible to learn how to move through the inner darkness of emotional difficulty, towards good mental health, and the Inner Spark of true contentment.

Several years ago one of my patients, Joan, shared a heartfelt confession with me. She was in tears when she told me that she was fed up and exhausted after struggling for what felt like years on end. She was burned out from work and was so drained that she thought she couldn't bear it any more. She had three children, and while her husband helped when he could, he was away often for work. Desperately she had been trying to juggle work, household, children, marriage . . . everything. It didn't help that she held herself to a high standard. This was how she came to see me, completely depleted of her life energy and having lost her will to live. She said she didn't want anything any more. She thought she couldn't manage to be here in this life, she felt like she couldn't hold the pain any longer. She shared her story looking me straight in the eye.

And then after a pause she said: 'But I wouldn't do it.' She wouldn't end her life. I asked her what was keeping her from ending her life, and she replied: 'My children. My family. My husband. My parents. No. I would never leave them behind like that. I want to live, I just don't want this suffering any more.' It was a very determined reply and I didn't doubt her for a second. As she spoke, her eyes came to life: a spark. There was an unmistakable spark of desire to be alive. A spark that helped her see herself in a bigger picture, as a meaningful and essential person to others. She saw that her suffering was something separate from who she truly was, and that – despite her emotional struggles and the feeling that she was drowning in her inner darkness – there was something in her that was willing to fight. She managed to connect to a deep inner motivation to move away from the inner darkness she had felt so consumed by. Feeling meaningful to her loved ones became her life raft in her lake of darkness. She wanted to live. She was motivated to find health and she was ready for change.

．．．

Did you know ...

that about one in three employees will experience burnout at some point? Burnout is a normal reaction to stress rather than a clinical diagnosis and is often used to describe stress disorders in relation to work. Burnout symptoms are a cluster of complaints related to mild depression and anxiety and are caused by increased exposure to stress over time. Burnout can occur when you are faced with stressors over which you have no control for extended periods of time. For instance, at work, due to financial issues or emotional pressure. This exposure causes exhaustion, while there is little to no opportunity to pause and recover. The recommended treatment or road to recovery includes psychotherapy and body-oriented therapies so as to reintegrate health simultaneously in multiple facets of your being. Psychotherapy will help you identify underlying causes such as patterns in thinking or behaviour related to your emotional wounds, and empower you to regain agency in your situation. In addition, taking a break and removing yourself from the stressors during your recovery is highly recommended. Practising attitudes of kindness and compassion towards yourself, through formal exercises such as mindful yoga and meditation, is considered both preventive and empowering. Receiving nutritional guidance in the form of functional medicine is also beneficial. If you think you may be burned out, be sure to check with your physician so that other conditions can be eliminated and so you can decide on the appropriate treatment.

. . . .

And this is how it is. The journey out of emotional struggle and away from the cognitive and behavioural patterns that are not serving us can only begin fully when we are ready to embrace the darkest thoughts and feelings we have. Acknowledging the presence of our most secret thoughts is the first step to freeing yourself. You need to let yourself make it personal – the inner dark is personal. The pain that you feel or the struggles you've experienced in your life, as an individual, are yours alone; only you know what it's like to embody these experiences. It is a very human experience to feel stuck in emotional hardship, so don't deny how dark things can feel. And it's just as human to desperately want the hardship and the darkness to disappear so you can feel free, happy, and joyous.

Wishing yourself well

A visualization practice

Before we set out on this journey of stepping out of struggle, I have an invitation for you. I am inviting you to work with yourself with the intention of understanding, to be aware and take care of yourself with gentleness, and to wish upon yourself goodness while making your way through this book. Perhaps you feel this invitation resonate immediately. And if you don't, that is all right too. This is a practice of self-compassion and even if you cannot feel it right now, maybe you can agree with yourself that you'll receive it sometime in the future.

1. **Take a seat**: Find a comfortable seat somewhere where there are few distractions. You can close your eyes if you like or rest your gaze softly on the floor.

2. **Kindness**: Repeat the following phrases to yourself silently or out loud. Repeat each of the phrases three times. Feel free to rephrase with words that resonate more deeply with you.

   - I wish for good health

   - I wish to be at emotional ease

   - I wish to treat myself with gentleness

   - I wish to be my own safe harbour of softness and kindness

3. **Contemplate**: After repeating these phrases three times each, sit for a moment, and see if you can notice how it feels to make these wishes for yourself.

4. **Return**: Finally, bring your attention to your body and to where you are sitting. Open your eyes and notice the room or space around you. And then, when you feel ready, come out of the seated posture and proceed with your day.

Integration

A practice of connecting the dots

The following exercise will integrate your experience from the 'Wishing yourself well' practice, above. By writing down your observations you begin to become aware of the truth of the experience. Keep your writing as descriptive as you can, and resist falling into the trap of analysing or explaining. This integration exercise returns throughout the book.

While wishing yourself well, was there anything that you noticed:

- Regarding your breath?
  For example: the rhythm. The depth. Change of quality. The difference between inhale and exhale. Please describe.

- In your body or connected to bodily sensations?
  For example: a sensation being intensely present. Some discomfort or comfort. One small area asking for all your attention, or a larger area of the body. Different sensations, some subtle, others obvious. Prickling, tickling, or temperature changes. Please describe.

- Regarding the activity of your mind or the movement of thoughts?
  For example: thoughts moving fast or slowly. One idea, thought, or situation demanding your attention. Or

were there many thoughts present, maybe scattered or jittery? Did you notice a shift in focus or attention? Did your quality of mind become clearer or more foggy? Please describe.

- In your emotions?
  For example: did you notice any emotion(s)? Did you notice any emotions arising and passing? Fading? Or perhaps you became aware of the intensity of emotions becoming stronger or lighter? Please describe.

Remember, try not to analyse your answers or to explain where sensations come from or why they are arising. Just notice what is present.

Make sure to read the *Wellbeing Prescription: Kindness* in the final chapter of the book, where function, dosage, and precautions are elaborated.

CHAPTER 2

Why Inner Spark?
Societal neurosis as the norm

We are all made of the same stardust, because literally everything is made of the same building blocks, these atoms within us. We also share the same spiritual journey, the living process of being created, becoming transformed, and then ceasing to exist . . .

It's not your fault

Our modern Western societies seem to value the success of the individual above all else. We are raised and groomed to be independent, to stand on our own two feet, to educate ourselves, and to perform and achieve. Yet even as our individuality is constantly fed and encouraged, the downside of being so self-centred is difficult to ignore. The focus on the individual creates a culture of constant comparison, feelings of loneliness, and even shame. We become alienated from each other within our communities. In this day and age our communities have become outwardly focused, overly individualized, and seemingly grounded in a form of collective neurosis. It is no surprise that the symptoms of these unhealthy times are affecting us.

Humans are social animals who thrive in herds (or

communities). It is often forgotten that our wellbeing is influenced by how we identify with respect to each other. A sense of belonging comes when we feel connected to our squad, our crew, the community we are at home with. It is within this community that we feel we have a purpose and where we have a meaningful function in relation to others. In social psychology this is known as in-group and out-group. In-group consists of those with whom we identify and feel we belong; out-group is everyone else. Often without realizing it, we express ourselves from this perspective through the many choices that we make: how we dress, talk, choose our words, what we engage in, what we don't engage in, and so forth. The mechanisms that drive us as social animals and invite us to define ourselves according to certain groups that we identify with are very strong. So strong that they may even make us do things that would be easy to criticize in hindsight. It is essential to understand that we may be quite unaware of the forces that drive us.

Not only are we social animals who strive to belong, we also strive towards the comfort of predictability. The ability to understand and predict our surroundings has been a vital force in evolution. The predictability we desire mostly has to do with the norms of the society in which we live and engage. Predictability means we can act appropriately and also correctly decode the behaviour of others. And this mechanism then affects our wellbeing.

It follows logically from this that we are greatly impacted by societal norms. With this in mind, it is important that we realize our generation expresses issues and conditions not only because of those generations who came before ours (as we tend to either embrace or rebel against the previous generations' norms) but also due to dominant movements in society.

Did you know . . .

that we thrive when there is interdependence but
not in solitude? The neuroscientist John Cacioppo
studied how our brains respond to loneliness and to
belonging. Feelings of belonging and community make
us strong, while feeling lonely makes us vulnerable,
weak, and sick. The individualistic focus of modern
society does very little to support interdependence
and relationships, and the subsequent decreased
feelings of belonging thus actually create pain and
fragmentation within us. More evidence of this is found
in a study undertaken by researchers Yang Claire Yang
et al., which found that social relationships are more
significant predictors of longevity than anything else.

. . . .

My great-grandmother harvested seaweed from the cold
Nordic sea, dried the seaweed, and fed it to her only cow so
that she could give her ten children milk to drink. She took
care of her children on her own while my great-grandfather
was out fishing in the wild ocean for months at a time. They
lived in a little oceanfront shack and she never knew whether
her husband would come home. When my grandmother
was little, she clung to her pregnant mother's hip while she
was out harvesting seaweed in that coldest of seas. Later,
during the Second World War, she married my grandfather.
They led an isolated life on their farm in Vikjorda. Their firstborn arrived soon after the war ended; five more children
followed. When the hardship of living on a small farm started
to take its toll, they decided to move to the regional capital,
Bodø. My grandfather set up a construction company and
the winds changed for them. Their income stabilized and

they were able to enjoy life a little more. When their children were grown and had left home, they decided to escape the darkest months of the Norwegian winter and spend time in Spain. During the span of her life my grandmother went from bare-bones survival on the Norwegian coast to sunny three-month holidays in Spain.

Industrialization had brought massive increases in productivity, and the effects were felt by the general population. There was a time of relative economic stability. So, as my grandparents were able to shift their focus after the Second World War from surviving to enjoying, my parents were able to grow up engaged and questioning the status quo of society and politics. Then came the millennials, my generation, born into the cradle of perfectionism. We wanted to do everything better. So much better. We thought we were able to do anything. We thought we could choose top-shelf options, and as a privileged generation the world seemed to be at our feet. So why then are we incarcerated in our controlling minds? Why are we stuck in the dance between ease and unease, sometimes to such an extent that not only is unease present but also dis-ease and dis-order. Why do our generations show the highest rates and earliest onset of mental health disease, when we are seemingly on top of everything else?

The problem

Today, performance and achievement have become status symbols. The norm in our society is to encourage perfectionism in every area possible. We become overwhelmed by our constant multitasking, and exhaustion symptoms and depletion become increasingly normal. Burnout and stress-related diseases are alarmingly common and still on the rise. Resourceful and intelligent people are running into walls, the madness of their daily functioning reducing them to pale, ineffective versions of themselves. Their Inner Spark has been suffocated – lost somewhere in the rubble of everything they feel they have to do in order to get where they want to go. Yet the paradoxical truth is that our knowledge around health is better than ever.

At times my life has felt just like riding my bike in rush-hour traffic through the middle of Amsterdam: I have to keep pedalling at the speed decided by the cyclists in front of me and behind me. If I don't keep up, I risk having someone crash into me and causing all sorts of chaos. And yet I know better than this. I know I should be able to untangle myself from this rat race. I am stuck between the desire to be part of it all and an aversion to the constant pressure. These conflicting feelings of desire and aversion have me tightly in their grip. Is there another way?

It is intense to grow up in a society and a time in which technological developments and the digitalization of our lives are so overwhelming. A time in which being busy, constant multitasking, and showing off our achievements are valued more than slow and simple living. While previous generations may have led more austere lives than ours in terms of general health, with more illness and shorter lifespans overall, their lives were simpler. There was a day-to-day steadiness to life that was less complicated in many ways than our lives today.

Biggie Smalls' 'Mo Money Mo Problems' comes to mind: more belongings, more problems; more alternatives, more problems. We may live in material abundance, but this is actually detrimental both to us and to our whole planet.

Shopping malls and online stores spew their wares at us, to be delivered to our doorstep by the very next day. We are led to believe we need these things, yet we don't. Certain platforms purporting to be spaces where we can connect with each other are actually the new lair of advertising's sharp claws, all aimed at creating new addictions in consumers. And the youngest among us have been digitally socialized, actually trained by social media platforms to react in specific ways. Like or dislike, kids are taught to react always with either desire or aversion, thus stimulating the need to have something else, something more, or something better. Or worse, fostering the insecurity that it would be better to be somebody else, somebody better. All of this strengthens beliefs of not being enough.

Digitalization may have sped life up, but from an evolutionary point of view our brains are still in hunter-gatherer times. So it is no surprise that slow living as a movement is on the rise, and I see this as a righteous reaction to all the speed. It makes perfect sense for folks to long for simplicity once again.

It is interesting to note that in parallel to the industrialization and then digitalization of our lives, science has come to mean more to many than religion and religious values. Spirituality has become a functional and individual affair. At the same time, we see an increase in mental health conditions such as anxiety, depression, and stress-related issues.

Post-industrialization has given us goal-driven lives where more is better, lives fuelled by mass consumption. Consequently there is massive overproduction that is leaving our planet with a defective ozone layer, melting polar ice caps and climate change, not to mention financial disruption, increasing wars, waves of refugees, and millennials cemented in the attitude of perfectionism. And since our younger generations are increasingly judged according to their cognitive efforts, achievements, and performance, they find they can't even rebel like their parents did in turning to sex, drugs, and rock 'n' roll. Instead of fighting against the status quo and taking to the streets, we see them taking a new approach: rebelling by becoming healthier than the healthiest, becoming environmentally conscious, and turning to yoga, meditation, and mindfulness in a desperate attempt to fill the emotional void that is eating them alive. And let's not forget that, in the midst of this, we are all fighting to find our passion and to fulfil our highest potential.

Nietzsche called this 'the religion of comfortableness'. An extreme illustration can be seen in the movie *The Matrix*, where humans are kept in pods, living in as stress-free an environment as possible, to be bred and fed so as to fuel and energize machines. It's hardly that far from the truth of social media, if you think about it: our attention and time online feed all sorts of algorithms, and perhaps in the future will feed AI too. Nietzsche wasn't optimistic, but he had a point: we do love being comfortable. He shrewdly observed that our desire for comfort would not diminish our suffering: 'If you stare long enough into the abyss, the abyss will stare back at you.'

Our struggle to somehow end the dance of joy and sorrow will in fact only create more suffering. The suffering comes when we choose not to engage in the dance of ease and unease, in the dance of our emotions. It comes when we don't know how to embody our inner dark skilfully, because we want above all to be comfortable. We are often quite scared of our emotions or scared of how they may express themselves in our lives and potentially interfere with whatever we are trying to achieve. We are addicted to the idea that happiness is the key. But we confuse happiness with comfort – material or financial. We believe if we can only get this or that, and not that and this, we'll be happy and life will be perfect. Every time we are not fulfilled in what we want or what we expect, we suffer. We may even believe there's something wrong with us. Something utterly and seriously, pathologically wrong. I've definitely asked myself that question a couple of times throughout my life. And I know most clients I have treated have asked themselves the same. Is there something wrong with me? Why am I stuck in this struggle? Am I beyond repair? Am I crazy?

One client said to me: 'Are you sure I'm not crazy?' Sarah had been suffering from panic attacks for a while, and even though her understanding of them had changed (she stopped believing the panic attacks would kill her), she was terrified of anyone seeing her while she had one. I asked why and she answered: 'Because then they would see with their bare eyes how crazily fucked up I am.' She was scared it would be revealed to the world that she was suffering from a mental health disease. I asked what the worst thing about that was, and she said: 'I'll be so full of shame. It'll be revealed that I cannot keep my shit together.'

There was nothing wrong with Sarah. And there's nothing wrong with you. This is human and it is normal. Our inner darkness causes suffering. The difficult thoughts. The so-called negative emotions. Sadness. Fear. Hurt. Insecurity. Anger. Jealousy. Loneliness. Hate. Shame. All as normal as normal can be. These emotions prove you are alive as a human being. To be able to emote is to feel and connect to the soul's creative expression. Emotions are a dance. The regulation of strain on the nervous system. A communication of the heart. Our non-verbal language of relating to other beings.

However we choose to define emotions, how we relate to them, how we embody them, express them, regulate them, and weave them into a meaningful story of our lives, is what is going to make all the difference. It is only when we understand our emotions and know how to express them that we can see they are just bits and pieces of who we are. They are not the whole of our being. We must therefore learn how to hold space for them and embody them fully. We must learn how we relate to them when they arise. Do we try to avoid them? Do we try to dull them? Do we try to distract ourselves by creating physical pain to deafen them? Or do we let ourselves drown in the waves of our emotions?

A contemporary spirituality

The predecessors of modern psychologists were soul counsellors, shamans, healers, and religious guides, so understandably non-Western philosophy was on many early psychologists' radars. Freud and Jung (among others) studied Eastern schools of thought and philosophy. Later, when psychology had been firmly accepted as a scientific field, the humanistic paradigm took over for pathology (focus on abnormality and illnesses), paving the way for positive psychology and the salutogenetic model (focusing on empowerment of health and wellbeing).

We already noted the possible connection between the decline in organized religious practices and the rise of mental health issues. We should also examine the connection here to yoga and wisdom teachings. We know that over the last few decades there has been huge growth in yoga, mindfulness, and similar experience-based practices. But why are we seeing such an increased interest in these practices? Why are so many secularized versions of Eastern and even mystic practices (like Kabbalah) drawing crowds, and why are so many people now willing to define themselves as 'spiritual but not religious'? Are these practices maybe a means to fill that religious void, functioning as individualized ways of practising spirituality? Role models like Oprah, Gwyneth Paltrow with Goop, Marianne Williamson, and Deepak Chopra have helped bring spiritual topics into the mainstream. And Western Buddhist teachers such as Pema Chödrön, Lama Tsultrim Allione, Jack Kornfield, Joseph Goldstein, and Sharon Salzberg have found a new way to share ancient teachings and create space for meditation practices in places like the Spirit Rock Meditation Center in California. Their students have in turn beautifully translated these teachings so they can be applied to contemporary psychology and into the healthcare system and treatments for both somatic and mental health. Jon Kabat-Zinn has secularized meditation with his mindfulness-based stress-reduction programme and helped bring this practice to those who are not interested in the spiritual side of meditation. And now centres for research, education, and the practice of compassion and mindfulness can be found at some of the most prestigious universities in the world, such as Stanford and Oxford.

Alongside the rise of Buddhist teachings in the West is the growing yoga community. While moving through yoga postures, practitioners are able to access mindfulness and self-compassion too; the movement becomes the meditation. Yoga has the potential to make mindfulness and awareness practices available to a variety of population groups. A great example is the Prison Yoga Project, which was set up by James Fox and can be found in prisons all over the world. Also yoga teachers like Jill Satterfield, Janice Gates, Anne Cushman, and Sarah Powers have united Eastern wisdom practices with movement practices and so brought these teachings to all corners of the globe.

In a parallel development, the clinical field of psychology has also experienced a clear paradigm shift over the past few decades and now increasingly values body-based practices as part of conventional treatment programmes. This has meant I have been able to bring yoga and mindfulness as experience-based practices directly into the work I do with my clients.

Why are people drawn to these practices, whether mindfulness meditations, more advanced compassion-based visualizations, or simple movements like mindful yoga? What is it that practitioners are finding? These formal practices (on a yoga mat or on a meditation cushion) first cultivate a focused attention in the practitioner. This focus is necessary so that later on in their practice the rising and passing of all phenomena, sensations, or objects of the mind can be observed. Students of these practices learn and experience directly that they are more than their worrying thoughts or their intense emotions.

This individualized spirituality is non-religious. While there may be spiritual practices in religion, spirituality in itself is a personal and subjective matter. Peterson and Seligman state that spirituality is universal and has intra-psychic functions. Spirituality refers to beliefs and practices that are grounded in the conviction that there is a transcendent (non-physical) dimension to life. And this spirituality then determines what people attribute meaning to and the ways they conduct relationships.

I believe spirituality is also about being courageous and willing to engage fully with this life and with your surroundings. Bringing spirituality into your life means you are willing to see yourself and the world – both the dark and the light – and you are willing to relate to it all. Like a photographer who harnesses the best possible light in landscape pictures, we shine a light onto ourselves by becoming still and turning towards our own inner landscapes.

So spirituality is not only a framework from which we come to understand our consciousness and existence, but it is also a way of engaging with life. Critics may counter that spirituality can become a crutch, or a way to externalize painful events. But when we use spirituality in this way we are actually guilty of spiritual bypassing, a term coined by John Welwood in 1983. The bypassing refers to the tendency some seekers have to use spiritual practices and understanding as a way of bypassing psychological wounds, patterns of interacting, thinking, and emoting, and thereby sidestepping deeply rooted, non-constructive behaviours.

From a psychological point of view, engaging in one's own emotional experience through meditation and as a spiritual practitioner is health-enhancing and a skilful way to acknowledge what you have agency over. Taking refuge in spiritual practice is actually a way to take charge of your own suffering. When pain becomes unbearable it can help to find something larger than yourself to turn to. And investigating and understanding our pain – and placing it in a context we can relate to through spiritual practice – is essential to alleviate suffering.

This helps explain why so many people take refuge in spiritual practices. A retreat into spirituality is a step back from the business of everyday life. It allows for observation of our own chaotic minds or feelings of being emotionally over-whelmed, and creates perspective by reminding us that we are not our thoughts, memories, emotions, or bodies, but so much more than that. And with this insight self-compassion and self-care become easier. Over time insights come and are experienced as sweetly as drops of honey, meaning is found, and inner conflict is resolved.

Empowering mental health and emotional wellbeing

Both during my studies and in my hospital practical training I shared mindfulness and mindful yoga (read: moving meditation) with various groups of patients. This was com-plementary to the multidisciplinary treatment programmes of conventional specialized mental healthcare. I worked with inpatient groups struggling with eating disorders such as anorexia nervosa and bulimia nervosa, and outpatient treatment programmes dealing with substance abuse and addiction. The group interventions were pilots and each round was evaluated with semi-structured interviews pre- and post-intervention.

The participants reported the following:

- They loved the group setting and that they could do something together without feeling the obligation to share anything, while simultaneously feeling encouraged to share if they wanted to.

- They appreciated learning from each other and hearing other participants' experiences of the practice, as this helped them normalize their own feelings and experiences.

- They loved moving. The gentle yoga movements and deep breathing were always appreciated.

- They loved learning about the breath and the nervous system and enjoyed feeling how deep breathing brought on a sense of ease.

- They felt encouraged to implement small lifestyle changes such as reducing daily smoking habits and paying more attention to the nutritional value of their food.

The overall conclusion was that these group sessions were valued positively by both in- and outpatient clients as a part of the psychiatric treatment they received.

As the popularity of yoga and mindfulness has sky-rocketed in recent decades, the body of research on these topics has also grown substantially. I define yoga as a moving meditation. Mindful yoga is a slow and flowing sequence of postures to the rhythm of calm breathing, and an observation and inquiry into what is experienced and noticed during the practice. This observation and inquiry are essential parts of the practice from a neurological perspective (more on this in Chapter 4). With the growing body of research, there is now an abundance of information regarding what works and what doesn't, and how and why. The scientific language employed in this research is functional as it is the language of our healthcare practices, and can soothe critical Western minds. But the essence is this: we see the Western scientific community confirming the wisdom of Eastern practices (derived from mystic traditions) in a very concrete way.

It is now fully accepted that these practices are beneficial to both physical and mental health and can contribute in treatment plans, alleviating many symptoms and complaints, and aiding in the healing process. Some effects are very specifically attributed to particular methods of practice, while other effects are less easily directly linked to a particular method. Below is a short summary of several of the effects; in no way is this an attempt to summarize the full scope of the research available.

Wisdom practices have psycho-educational value

We can learn about ourselves and about our psyche from practising because the underlying philosophy of these practices promotes the acceptance of inner restlessness, of emotional struggle, and of mental suffering. Through its focus on kindness towards oneself it then builds skills in practitioners to deal with this inner turmoil, and it becomes an accessible tool on the path to healing. It speaks to many: it's transcultural, trans-religious, and all-encompassing, and it therefore resonates with simply being human. In addition it is an experiential-based practice and teaches us to become aware of sensations related to various phenomena as they arise and shift in quality and intensity. These practices show us that we can quiet our minds and that we can deliberately shift our internal focus of attention. This then stimulates a broader perspective, allowing us to experience that we are more than our physical sensations, more than our thoughts, more than our emotions.

Lifestyle changes and self-care

There is a clear difference between the short- and long-term effects of the cluster of exercises defined as formal meditative practices. This cluster includes the full spectrum of a yoga practice: asana, concentration exercises, meditation, and breath work known as pranayama. Since most research on these practices has been carried out in efficacy studies (does it work and how well?), much remains to be done in studying the longitudinal effects, looking at effects and factors over more extended periods of time. Lifetime studies, for instance, and studies over generations are rare. Yet we do know one thing about the long-term effects of a spiritual or yoga practice, and that has to do with major, often important, lifestyle changes. Yoga and mindfulness have been shown to inspire people to reconsider lifestyle choices and take responsibility towards changing their ways when it comes to their personal health. We therefore conclude that yoga and mindfulness are health-promoting practices. Overall, an increased awareness of what serves our health and what doesn't arises. And the ability to recognize our own patterns of thinking, emoting, and behaving improves. To what degree one is able to take action and then integrate the changes in the long term has not been sufficiently researched yet. But one of the things that stands out, at least in the short term, is dietary changes. Practitioners are found to eat more healthily and to more often choose a plant-based diet. An increase in regular exercise is evident as the movement through yoga asana sequences becomes more routine, and this has an effect on the strength and flexibility of muscles, the health of deeper and connective tissues, and general joint health. The effects of breath work, the pranayama practice, work towards toning the nervous system. And working so intimately with the breath has been shown to help people cut down and even give up smoking completely. In fact, it helps reduce the intake of all toxic substances. A regular practice over time therefore promotes a variety of positive lifestyle changes and brings an awareness of the body and mind, and this leads to healthier choices that benefit the practitioners' daily life.

Practising precaution

When discussing the benefits of yoga and mindfulness, which can be unwisely recommended for most things between heaven and earth, it is important to recognize that these practices are not always a good idea when it comes to mental health. Even though yoga benefits physical and mental health greatly, in no way are we to assume that all yoga benefits everyone in this way. And although all yoga contains elements of mindfulness (that is, paying attention to what arises and passes in a given moment, with gentleness and understanding, pausing the critical inner voice), not all yoga choices are made mindfully! For instance, Ashtanga Vinyasa yoga is not recommended for those struggling with eating disorders due to the fact that it may trigger deeply seated ritualistic behaviour and perfectionism. Similarly yin yoga or mindfulness meditation are rarely recommended for those dealing with severe depressive episodes. For those unfamiliar with these kinds of yoga, Ashtanga yoga is a vigorous and dynamic movement practice, whilst yin yoga and mindfulness meditation are practices that invite practitioners into silence and expose them to their inner landscapes much more than dynamic practices do. Dynamic practices often require more instruction and thus hold the attention of the practitioner in the moment, while silent practices leave the practitioner more to their roaming mind. The latter is not always helpful to a patient who is stuck in ruminating thoughts and emotions, as is usually the case in severe depressive episodes. For more on precautions, read the Wellbeing Prescriptions in the final chapter or join one of my courses.

The brain and the nervous system

Research has shown that meditation leads to an increase in grey matter in the brain and reduces the size of ventricles (the cavities where cerebrospinal fluid is produced). These cavities are relatively large in brains exposed to years of mental health disease and disorder, and relatively small in long-term practitioners of meditation. These are exciting findings as they support the evidence that these practices stimulate neuroplasticity, the brain's capacity to develop and regenerate. Other studies show increased amounts of positive neurotransmitters, which accounts for yoga's positive effects on moods and anxiety issues. And though we cannot conclude that meditation or yoga on their own can treat mood disorders, we can be sure that these practices reduce levels of unease related to anxiety. Some studies also show that mindfulness-based practices stimulate better emotional tolerance and regulation, which is beneficial in strengthening coping mechanisms and in dealing with stress. Many studies additionally show that these practices stimulate a lower heart rate variability (HRV), which increases parasympathetic toning and puts the practitioner at ease. For those of you who have practised yoga or mindfulness, you may be familiar with that post-practice glow. In particular the breathing tones the parasympathetic activation of the nervous system to such an extent that HRV is stabilized. Deep, slow, yogic breathing, or diaphragmatic breathing with prolonged exhales, has also been shown to tone the vagus nerve and thereby stimulate parasympathetic activation. This means we can step on the brakes that are built into our stress-activating inner alarm system. Breathing tones the vagus nerve and this slows down our stress response system. The polyvagal theory was pioneered by Stephen Porges, should you be interested in learning more about it. If you are more interested in practising with this, I recommend *The Breathing App* (it's free) for resonance breathing, created by yogi Eddie Stern, the well-known mindfulness instructor Deepak Chopra, and the musician Moby (among others). And you'll find a simple breathing practice at the end of the next chapter.

We've discussed the method-specific effects, but how about the non-specific effects? There are several non-specific factors that are difficult to control in studies of the above-mentioned practices, yet these are bound to have an impact on the outcome. I borrow terminology from Bruce Wampold and his work in psychotherapy, but I find it applicable and relevant here. Examples of non-specific factors are *the skills* of the teacher sharing the practices – how they embody and convey the experience; the *relationship quality* between the teacher and student/practitioner – mutual openness, interest, and respect appear to be of utmost importance; the *motivation* of the student and to what extent the student/practitioner *believes* in the method. To reclaim your Inner Spark it is vital you recognize what you can do yourself, as this will increase the benefits of such practices. To what extent you believe in these methods is for you to know; however, the fact that you are sitting with this book in your hands probably affirms at least some belief. Regarding your motivation, which is a complex and delicate topic, we'll explore more on this in Chapter 6.

A challenge when discussing research on meditative practices and yoga comes from the enormity of the subject matter. These practices are varied and are grounded in a range of philosophical schools. They encompass myriad practices from long seated meditations to prostrations, to sweat-breaking sun salutations in tiger-patterned leotards, to sometimes very challenging breathing techniques, to fasting, to ethics of behaviour, and so on. Studies are primarily done on contemporary practices, consisting of movement, concentration, and breath practices in various combinations. Yet the studies are limited in their strength due to the limited populations within which they can even be conducted, so it may be premature to draw generalized conclusions at this point. Also short-term programmes and studies may not say as much as we'd like about long-term effects. Still, as the past decade has already seen a huge growth in this body of research, I'm confident that more exciting research and results are on their way.

Based on my own experience and on the growing amount of research, there is not a doubt in my mind that yoga and mindfulness are immensely important when considering all-round and general interventions towards more emotional wellbeing and integrated health. I am a strong advocate of bringing yoga and mindfulness into the sphere of general healthcare, and would love to see it implemented more frequently as a green prescription for prevention and recovery. But I also want to see meditation teachers and yoga therapists included in multidisciplinary teams for treatment of mental health. Hopefully in the future these experience-based practices will also be widely shared in prisons, in schools, and as an essential component of education.

It is impossible, however, to consider individual health without inquiring into the reality of your immediate surroundings. And even though these practices can offer short-term release, they are no quick fix. Their true strength comes from their power to stimulate a practitioner towards lifestyle changes, and to support you as you find agency in your life, and work towards a more balanced daily existence. These practices are empowering. And interestingly the research on yoga and mindfulness shows that it is not necessarily the actual practices that bring about change, but the fact that they shift the attitude of practitioners, who then move themselves towards that change.

On being patient

In order to step out of any struggle, which is a process, it is essential that you consider patience. As I embark on a psychotherapeutic journey with my clients, I always invite them to be patient. I ask my clients if they are willing to take things one step at a time. If they are to commit to being supported, and guided, then patience is a first step towards compassion for yourself. And as we saw in the previous chapter, compassion or kindness is something we can practice. It may feel counterintuitive because, when we are faced with challenging times, impatience often occurs. We quite naturally want the pain or discomfort to disappear, we want to instantly feel better, we want to feel comfortable (again). Yet there's no point in forcing anything; patience is key. I'll return to this and discuss exactly how we can expand our patience skills in Part II.

For now, ask yourself this question: are you willing to commit and become your own client in this process of tidying up your inner chaos and reclaiming your Inner Spark?

Connecting with yourself

A practice of concentration

This Nudge to Action is an invitation to connect to yourself in this moment. It's not always easy, and perhaps you'll encounter something you don't expect or notice something you don't want to, but it's useful. See this exercise as a kind embrace, like a dear friend would greet you, asking you how you are actually doing in this moment.

This exercise will take you 5–10 minutes, but feel free to sit for up to 30 minutes. It allows you to connect to yourself, here and now, in body, mind, heart, and breath. You can do this practice every day or whenever you need to connect to yourself.

1. **Take a seat**: Take a comfortable seat. Make sure your lower back, hips, and knees are supported. You can close your eyes if you like or rest your gaze softly on the floor.

2. **The body**: First allow your attention to move through your body for a couple of moments. From where the legs and sit bones connect with the ground (cushion, floor, or chair), up through your upper body, to the very top of your head. Perhaps you can also feel the back of your body, and the front.

3. **The breath**: Then move your attention to your breath. Can you feel your breath in this moment? Can you feel the air moving in and out of the nostrils? For the

next few moments, feel the quality of your breath in the here and now.

4. **The mind**: Move your attention further inwards to the movements of your thoughts. Without paying particular attention to any specific thoughts or ideas, see if you can observe the quality of your mind right now, as if you were watching water in a river passing you by.

5. **The emotions**: When sitting here connecting to your inner self, perhaps you notice emotions floating by, or arising and passing. Can you notice the degree of intensity these emotions hold? Try not to go into the particularities of the emotions or to get carried away by them, but do try to notice whether they feel pleasant, unpleasant, or something in between.

6. **Return to the body**: Feel your breath. Feel the inhalation and exhalation moving in and out of your nostrils. Feel the breath moving in your body. Feel your body. The back and the front. From your legs and sit bones to the very top of your head.

7. **Come back**: Take a couple of deeper breaths. And when you feel ready, open your eyes.

8. **Reflect**: Take a few moments to inquire, and write down in a few key words what you noticed while doing this exercise. There may be different things to notice each time you do this.

See the following practice of observation on how to connect the dots of your experience, and how to integrate what you have engaged in.

. . . .

Integration

A practice of connecting the dots

While engaging in the above exercise, was there anything
that you noticed:

- Regarding your breath?
  *For example: the rhythm. The depth. Change of
  quality. The difference between inhale and exhale.
  Please describe.*

- In your body or connected to bodily sensations?
  *For example: a sensation being intensely present. Some
  discomfort or comfort. One small area asking for all
  your attention, or a larger area of the body. Different
  sensations, some subtle, others obvious. Prickling,
  tickling, or temperature changes. Please describe.*

- Regarding the activity of your mind or the movement
  of thoughts?
  *For example: thoughts moving fast or slowly. One idea,
  thought, or situation demanding your attention. Or
  were there many thoughts present, maybe scattered or
  jittery? Did you notice a shift in focus or attention? Did
  your quality of mind become clearer or more foggy?
  Please describe.*

- In your emotions?
  *For example: did you notice any emotion(s)? Did you
  notice any emotions arising and passing? Fading? Or*

perhaps you became aware of the intensity of emotions becoming stronger or lighter? Please describe.

Remember, try not to analyse your answers or try to explain where sensations come from or why they are arising. Just notice what is present.

Make sure to read the *Wellbeing Prescription: Patience* in the final chapter of the book, where function, dosage, and precautions are elaborated.

CHAPTER 3

What is Inner Spark?
Appreciating the ebb and flow

Wanderer. Of valleys and great forests. Of majestic mountains and deep lakes. Of the land of 1,000 suns and 1,000 moons. Of the dancing Northern Lights. Of the icy oceans, with life in all the colours of the rainbow. Of the starry darkness and silent storms. Of never-ending summer days. Of this mighty nature. You belong to it. You are it. You are stardust, like everything in it. You are not its master. Nor there to be entertained by it. You are allowed to visit. To take part. Humbly. See how it all arises and passes. The seasons. The light. The beings. You.

The ebb and flow

Growing up in the Arctic Circle, where nature is vast and the weather is mighty, it was easy to experience myself as a tiny being in a larger context, and being so fully exposed to this nature gave rise to some serious questions early in my life. Existential questions like 'what is our purpose here?' and 'what is God?' arose naturally while I lay on the moss-covered Norwegian ground, gazing up at the vastness of the northern skies. This questioning evolved with time into a deep desire to understand how we function as human beings. I decided to study psychology, the science of understanding the human animal. I took courses in a wide variety of subjects ranging from social psychology, neuropsychology and the brain's composition and functioning, to organizational psychology and group processes, to clinical psychology and the treatment of disease and disorder. Alongside this, I dedicated myself to learning about spiritual practices, ranging from the religious traditions of my childhood to the mysticism of yogic mythology and Buddhist simplicity. All of this brought me to discover what Inner Spark is.

Life is challenging and it tosses us around in the ebb and flow of ease and unease. At times the intensity of the pain caused by life's challenges increases to the point where it becomes a chronic presence of emotional and/or mental suffering. The yogis discovered thousands of years ago that there's a way out of this suffering and they believed that it is the ruminating mind holding us captive in its prison that is causing our distress. The way out of this prison is to observe the phenomena of your mind in the actual moment when they arise and pass. When we do this we realize that there is an ebb and flow to them and that all pains evolve and transcend. We realize also that the only way to truly relate to this is by allowing ourselves to be in direct contact with what arises. We must tolerate what arises in order to overcome. We must accept so we may overcome. The key is to not avoid the truth of our experience.

The rabbit and the universe

I have two young boys, and the pain of giving birth was beyond anything I could imagine. Yet at the same time their births were also the most grounding and in-the-moment experiences I have had. I felt humbled in the realization that there was nothing I could do, that my body was doing its own thing. This birthing was beyond the mind, it was a form of instinctual magic!

As my firstborn grew through infancy I was mesmerized. Looking into his eyes, I felt like I was looking into a gateway to the universe. I imagined when looking into my little boy's eyes (at that moment still developing his sight, only able to see contrasting shapes in my nearby face) that he was directly connected to the here and now, exactly as any adult meditator strives to be. It made me think of a story by Jostein Gaarder I read as a teenager. The story goes something like this: imagine a big, fluffy rabbit floating in the universe. When babies are born, they are born on the very tip of the rabbit's fur, looking the universe straight in the eye. They are as intimately connected as possible. As the babies start to learn sounds, words, and their meanings, as they start to form emotions and thoughts, as they learn to experience time and space, the human brain is conditioned. Little by little as the child learns it crawls further and deeper into the rabbit's fur. It becomes an infant, a toddler, a child, and a teenager. By the time the baby reaches adulthood, it will have moved all the way down into the warmth of the rabbit's fur, and settled in against its body where life is comfortable, predictable, and safe.

This story illustrates how in adulthood our minds are less flexible than when we are born, and how our upbringing has conditioned us. That which is known to us is familiar and therefore at least perceived to be predictable. It doesn't matter if what is known serves us well or not, whether it is beneficial to us or perhaps detrimental to our health. What matters is that it is familiar and predictable, which is always our preference. This is because from an evolutionary perspective, that which is known or predictable will increase our odds for survival. Changing our behaviours is therefore difficult. It is, however, possible, though we must realize that change needs to come from the inside. Real change literally requires a shift in the chemical activity of our brains. For this kind of real and powerful change to happen, our motivation must be very sincere and very deep. This may explain the allure of yogic practices, as these give us hope that we can move out of the comfort of the rabbit's fur and see that direct connection to the universe in its purest form. We'll return to the matter of readiness for change, and actionable steps, in Chapter 6.

The conditioning of our minds, which on the one hand so beautifully allows us to learn, to grow and mature, and become autonomous adults, on the other hand causes our downward spiral deep into the dark comfort of the rabbit's fur. The familiarity of what is known and predictable leads us to believe we are thriving. Familiar situations also keep us in our neurochemical comfort zone. Even if our habits or perspectives are not serving us well, we hold onto them so that our brain's chemicals can fire up as we expect them to. Until, suddenly, the inevitable happens: we are exposed to some unpredictable event, something new that feels uncomfortable. This activates our body's alarm system and we feel a stress response. This is a good sign! This means the mechanisms of your alarm system work. However, in some cases the triggers are too intense, and in such situations we may feel stuck rather than encouraged into a movement or response. When our stress response is activated, many outcomes are possible. At worst, we get stuck in the experience and we hold onto it as if it is the truth.

A major sign of being stuck is fear. When we feel scared of something new or when we fear that our feelings aren't right, we start to believe something needs to change. And when this happens we get caught in a malicious cycle driven by the forces of desire and aversion. We find ourselves spiralling, faster and faster, the grip of the discomfort becoming tighter and tighter. We resist more and more, and we only feel more and more stuck. In fact, we are stuck in the fear of leaving the warmth of the rabbit's fur. We fear what might happen if we let go of what we know. We must let go of the conditioned patterns that are a result of our upbringing, we must let go of emotional patterns and of behaviours. But this is stressful because abandoning what we know means stepping into the unknown. This is unpredictable, and from our instinctual perspective therefore possibly even dangerous. Arriving right back on the tip of the fur feels like our worst-case scenario, way out of our comfort zone. What if we move off the fur completely, floating into the nothingness of the space beyond the rabbit? This is our ultimate fear: non-existence.

From an evolutionary perspective our instinct is to hold onto that which is familiar and known, and this may be what has kept our species alive throughout the course of time. But the world is not what it was; we don't need our caveman instincts like we used to. Our contemporary lives do not regularly require us to detect fight-or-flight situations or to rely on the other skills our brains and nervous systems previously excelled in. We arguably need very different skills now than when we were fending for our lives in the wilderness. These days our sensory systems are almost constantly exposed to input on a nearly unimaginable scale; we are constantly being triggered. Emotional competence is more essential than ever. Yet stepping out of emotional struggle requires the unravelling and examination of difficult emotions and for us to properly learn how to embody and tolerate our emotions.

In addition to understanding ourselves, we must hone our people skills and put effort into understanding other people's minds if we are to survive happily in this densely populated and socially connected world.

Qualities of being and wellbeing

I differentiate between what I call 'the qualities of being' and wellbeing. These qualities are determined by the intensity of the emotional states that we experience, and they are reflected in our ability to function – on a psychological, physical, and social level.

For example, most people want to know how to step out of struggle. To answer that, we must understand what we need and when we need it, in relation to our mental health and our overall functioning. In order to understand these needs I have designed a model and a descriptive overview of our qualities of being in relation to the intensity of the experienced difficulty.

One thing we know for sure is that life has its challenges. It is useful to focus on emotional struggles and mental health in this model, as this is most often what motivates people to look into Eastern wisdom teachings. They are attracted to these practices' promise to help them transcend suffering and find and sustain ease. The qualities of being range from *sukkha* (Pali for 'joy') to *dukkha* (Pali for 'suffering') as referred to in Dharma teachings. Or from ease to unease, and then to disease and disorder.

The following diagram shows the qualities of being and portrays their similarities with the tolerance window as applied in trauma theory. The window of tolerance refers to a state of ease in which we are able to regulate ourselves skilfully, act wisely, and where our brains are able to make informed choices. As intense stressors or more bothersome symptoms increase, we act less skilfully and become disconnected from parts of the brain responsible for informed decision-making. This affects us on many levels, not just emotionally. We lose the ability to hit the brakes on our nervous system too, and even the endocrine system (where hormones maintain homeostasis) is affected and can become distressed. Triggers may be at the chemical, environmental (including relational), or physical level. Whatever the reasons for this distress, the expression of each quality of being appears to involve the whole of our bodily systems.

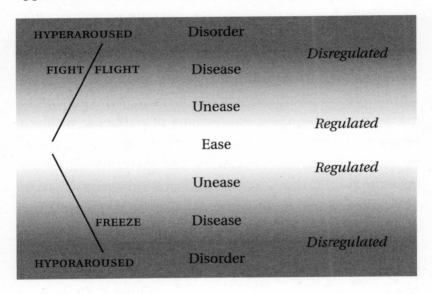

HYPERAROUSED	Disorder	
		Disregulated
FIGHT / FLIGHT	Disease	
	Unease	
		Regulated
	Ease	
		Regulated
	Unease	
FREEZE	Disease	
		Disregulated
HYPORAROUSED	Disorder	

This model makes it clear when we can benefit most from wisdom teachings. Of course, anyone with an interest can practise and, as mentioned, there are multiple psycho-educational benefits to be found in the practices. However, the higher the symptom pressure, the more challenging it will be to practise. That is why research concerned with clinical efficacy points primarily to these practices in the prevention and recovery phases.

Each quality of being is defined by the intensity and the presence of symptoms. High-intensity symptoms cause a significant decrease in daily functioning, and the presence of bothersome symptoms can disturb thinking and behaviour to such an extent that taking care of oneself and one's health becomes impossible. In this model, *ease* is the highest form of wellbeing, and *disorder* the poorest. This wellbeing is expressed in a person's ability to take care of their basic needs, such as personal hygiene, food, a place to live, clothing, and so forth. Pain or suffering may inhibit a person from going to work or school, or maintaining a social life. It is not uncommon for it to disturb sleep and food intake. In cases where the presence or intensity of these symptoms is high, we speak of disorder, implying that there is a more chronic presence and expression of pain. It is possible to fluctuate between these expressions of wellbeing within a lifetime, and both the frequency and the intensity depend on our genes, personal resources, and the environment we grew up in.

Below are the qualities of being, in order of how intensely they are experienced; how they affect our ability to function:

- **Ease** – a state of wellbeing. Contentedness is dominant, *sukkha* offers a gentle veil that allows you to see the world and yourself with a soft and compassionate gaze. You are able to engage fully in health-promoting activities and behaviour. You are able to differentiate between what serves you and what doesn't, and you are able to act accordingly.

- **Unease** – a state of being in which wellbeing is interrupted by homeostatic intervals that are not quite in balance. There may be disruptions in sleep, appetite, or a general sense of imbalance. Symptoms like thought rumination and anxiousness begin to present, especially when you feel tired or low on energy. A feeling that becoming overwhelmed is imminent. General levels of functioning have started to decrease. You are less capable of choosing behaviours and setting boundaries that serve you.

- **Disease** – a state of being in which symptoms become more frequent, and your general levels of functioning (in relation to work, school, or social life) have decreased significantly. You suffer from longer periods of not feeling like your normal strong self, you are not able to function as you wish, and *dukkha* holds you tightly in its grip. Anxiousness feels omnipresent and dense, you feel continuous fear, and you may have panic attacks. Ruminating repetitive thoughts spiral downhill and drag you into the dark depths of doubt. You suffer from a lack of initiative, ambivalent feelings, and a sense of meaninglessness.

- **Disorder** – a state of being in which symptoms are chronic and constantly present. They may even feel like personality traits, deeply embedded patterns that affect your functioning every day, perhaps over years, perhaps since childhood or early adulthood. The intensity of the symptoms is also more or less constant. The pressure you experience is crippling, and survival is your main goal. Causes may be plentiful, triggers varied, and whatever happens seems to intensely affect your life and your ability to live without help or support.

There is no doubt we can learn new skills in order to embody pain or bothersome symptoms with more ease and less suffering. Neuroplasticity confirms that we can change our behaviour, our ways of thinking, and the way we hold space for the inner darkness of our most difficult and turbulent emotions. And we can start by stepping towards a new way of being with ourselves, with our surroundings, and with how we navigate our way through this world. A Buddhist proverb offers hope: 'Pain is part of living; suffering is optional.' This is a hopeful reminder of the truth: that we can indeed learn to understand and be with pain and emotional struggle in a different way. We can acknowledge pain skilfully. We must remind ourselves that we can learn how to lead our lives in more sustainable ways with more contentedness and well-being.

What Inner Spark is

Now that we've looked into the rabbit's fur, moved with the ebb and flow of ease and unease, imagined ourselves in direct contact with the actual moment, and discovered the qualities of being, it is time to define Inner Spark.

Inner Spark is the essence of who you are. It is a state of wellbeing created by you courageously moving through the lake of your inner dark. Inner Spark is where your sense of purpose, hope, and meaning resides. It is a quality of your soul, or the essence of who you are as an individual. It is where you exist free from the grip of your conditioning. Where you are at ease, the majority of the time. We connect to our Inner Spark when we move through difficult emotions and challenging times. It is in this motion, initiated by our own agency, that transcendence is sparked. When we align with our inner dark, Inner Spark is ignited. As we reach new levels of awareness and see how the patterns of our thinking and emotions play out in our bodies and behaviour, we ready ourselves to choose that which serves us better, whether in relationships, in situations, or in self-care choices. It is the continuous willingness to embrace yourself fully and to see that you are more than your isolated thoughts, emotions, and sensations. You are a mosaic of continuously moving parts, a dynamic unity. Inner Spark is also the ability hold your whole self in compassion and understanding, tolerating the parts of yourself that you may not like very much. In the moments in which you are able to be with your darkness, you will come to see yourself differently. Allowing yourself to embrace the harsher sentiments you feel towards yourself will lead you to a place of gentleness.

Inner Spark is when you live your life from this space of gentleness, free from the conditioning of the mind. And this is what yogis used their practices for, to attain this radical freedom, liberating themselves from the suffocating grip that the conditioned mind has on us. (I'm aware the term 'radical freedom' was coined by existential philosophers, but I will leave a discussion on free will out of this book.) Contemporary psychotherapy is grounded in the same belief – that we can have a higher quality of life when we learn to stop acting and living based on our preconditioned assumptions and core beliefs. We can learn to free ourselves from thoughts based in fear and from controlling behaviours that are an attempt to shut down negative emotions. Such a shutdown only works to strengthen unhealthy emotional struggles and is counterproductive. Wisdom practices and schools of thought have known this for centuries and can be seen as the first institutes of cognitive sciences. Their premise was radical in their time, as they claimed that it was possible to free ourselves from how we perceive the world.

Inner Spark is when you can access and cultivate strong emotional and wholesome mental health over time. A capacity of tolerance, where you can hold space for yourself and your heart (read: difficult emotions), and from there hold space for others.

....

Did you know ...
that four elements are valued above all else when defining what a meaningful life is, according to journalist and researcher of positive psychology Emily Esfahani Smith? Her work revealed that a meaningful life depends on belonging, purpose, transcendence, and storytelling.

....

What do you need for your Inner Spark to shine?

Joy and a sense of wellbeing are present when we feel our lives have a deeper meaning and when we feel there's a balance between ease and unease. As we saw in the previous chapter, humans are social animals. We thrive best in herds, as we have the best chance of survival when we travel in packs. We are stronger together, and research confirms how our health deteriorates when we're feeling lonely. Feeling that we belong to a herd, a group, that we have our role or function within a community, or simply that we have someone near us to share life with makes a significant difference in the quality of our lives and in the quality of being, as discussed earlier in this chapter. Having meaningful relationships and a healthy social network can help us greatly in moving towards a connection to our Inner Spark.

The first person we need to build a strong and healthy relationship with is ourselves. Being compassionate and understanding towards yourself will help you develop compassionate and emotionally healthy connections with others. Belonging includes meaning something to someone, so naturally our relationships affect the quality of our being directly. Thoughts of how we can mean something to someone start to develop early in our lives. How our parents or caregivers mirror us through their emotional responses to us sets the blueprint for how we carry ourselves later in life when we meet and interact with others. It sets the foundation for how we trust, how we read those around us, how we choose to behave and respond, and how we position ourselves within a group.

Another way for our Inner Spark to shine is when what we've experienced (however painful) – and how we feel about that experience with hindsight – begins to take on some kind of meaning to us. As we retell our stories, if we can bring the events together towards some meaningful moment, connecting the dots within a bigger picture and a larger life story, then our lives come together fully and start to make sense to us. You might find some meaning that resonates with your values or you might find insights into how you understand and know yourself. The story of who you are and what you experience becomes meaningful when all the dots are connected into wholeness. Feeling that what we experience has a purpose – not only in our own lives but also within the context of being human – gives ease. Contemporary spiritual movements can help us find this way of thinking and looking at ourselves. They may teach us also that knowing how we feel or what we experience isn't a separate or fragmented experience at all – it is intensely human. This brings ease because it confirms that what we are going through or have gone through is within the realm of a normal human life. We see there is nothing wrong with us. We no longer feel detached or separate from others. On the other hand, when we define ourselves as abnormal or believe that our experience is different from what others might experience, we set ourselves apart and isolate ourselves, at least mentally. The process of disconnecting from our surroundings has started with just this thought. And feeling disconnected creates more unease. A much stronger approach is to recognize when you fall into thoughts of separation, and then to look instead for thoughts of unification.

There is no doubt that ease and a sense of wellbeing need to be present to connect to your Inner Spark. But even in challenging times, I believe finding ease within unease is always an option. This means that Inner Spark is always within reach, even when you doubt it. Moving from emotional struggle to Inner Spark requires us to transition or, shall we say, transcend from one state (unease) to the other (ease). This requires a significant shift in our perspective and involves the above-mentioned framework of perceived meaningfulness. A shift like this happens when we have gathered enough drops of insight in our honeypot. How and where do we find these honey drops? By embracing the darkness of emotional struggle. As my teachers at Spirit Rock would say: 'By sitting with it. Sit with yourself, with all your pain, in courage. Don't become it. Don't let it overwhelm you.

Allow it to arise. And to pass. Hold it. Gently. And you'll find yourself immersed in the moment and in the state of flow, as Mihaly Csikszentmihalyi defined it.' You can even find flow in the struggle when you're fully immersed in what you're doing, like sitting gently with pain.

Of course, sitting with the discomfort like this will take some practice. You cannot learn the techniques quickly in an online course and then expect emotional pain or struggles to be a thing of the past. But the good news is that, once you have learned the method, release is within your reach. It's like riding a bicycle: when you know how it works, you don't forget. Through this new knowledge and insight, you can recognize when challenging times arrive or unease begins to build inside of you, and you immediately have at your disposal very potent tools to tackle the issue. If you'd like to begin sitting with your pain and discomfort, first you'll need to learn to focus your attention (one-pointed concentration). Then you must learn about the practice of meditation. And finally with this you'll learn how to embrace whatever arises with mindfulness, holding yourself with compassion. You can simply and gently become the observer and the container of whatever is present.

There is an incredible life force that runs through us. This force moves us forward even when we are faced with challenges in our lives. As we move forward through our challenges, we find ourselves building emotional and mental resilience. We become masters of our own lives, and we experience this kind of mastery as small victories, or maybe big ones like being able to sit with pain. The mastery over our own fate and life and the victories battling the darker days give us resilience, and this strengthens the light of Inner Spark. A practice won't make us immune to emotional struggles; we must accept these as a part of being human and of this beautiful life. But our spiritual practice will help us face all aspects of life with confidence. It strengthens us by helping us become more flexible, more spontaneous, more at ease, more loving to ourselves, and more compassionate to others. This mastery is the magic threshold of transcendence, and it can be felt in the moment when that which was unknown and felt unattainable has become known and feels accomplishable.

Life is a wondrous journey in which we discover the conditionings of our mind. We begin to recognize those conditionings as we approach the edge of our comfort zones, and naturally we try to overcome these conditionings and find new, lighter ways of being. Sometimes we succeed. Sometimes we don't. Either way, befriending your inner dark allows you to embody whatever arises gently, with understanding and compassion, and from this space you can embody yourself with greatness. You can live from your Inner Spark.

Feeling your breath

A simple breathing practice

In this Nudge to Action I invite you to connect directly to your breath. 'The air of spirit matter, the life force energy, where soul resides and lives in the embodied earthly form of the physical body.' Research shows that of all practices, whether in meditation or yoga, breathing is very effective in calming the stress response of the nervous system. If practised regularly, aware breathing can help you find ease when in a state of unease.

This exercise is a great way to find focus for your mind, especially when the mind feels jumpy and chaotic. Practising this regularly will help you ground and centre yourself, and let you take a gentle break for the body and the heart when life starts to feel intense or overwhelming. Think of this as a way to keep your emotional stamina toned. It is not recommended you do this practice when you feel an anxiety attack building. It is better to practise when at ease to increase resilience.

1. **Take a seat**: Find a comfortable seat, or if you prefer you could also stand on both feet. In that case, find a steady, comfortable stance.

2. **Turn inwards**: If you like, you can close your eyes, or rest your gaze softly on one spot.

3. **Settle**: After settling into your pose, take a couple of deep breaths.

4. **Observe the breath**: Bring your attention to your breath. Can you feel your own breath in this moment? Can you notice the quality of your breath in this moment? For example, can you notice the rhythm of the inhale and exhale? Perhaps they differ in length and depth? Can you observe the air moving by itself, without you needing to do anything, in and out of your nostrils?

5. **Anapanasati (focus on breathing)**: Silently repeat as you breathe: 'I'm breathing in. I'm breathing out. Breathing in, breathing out.' Do this following the pace of your natural breath, without trying to control it. Focus your attention fully on the breath: 'In. Out. In. Out.'

6. **Resonance breathing**: You may like to count as you inhale and exhale, for example counting four on the in breath and six on the out breath, or use a count on inhale and exhale that feels right to you (following your own inner pace as you count). Continue like this for the next 5–10 minutes.

7. **Return**: Then return your attention to your body. Notice your whole body, from your feet to the top of your head. Notice the front and back of your body.

8. **Open your eyes**: Take a couple of deep breaths. If you had your eyes closed, open them gently.

Integration

A practice of connecting the dots

While engaging in the above exercise, was there anything that you noticed:

- Regarding your breath?
  For example: the rhythm. The depth. Change of quality. The difference between inhale and exhale. Please describe.

- In your body, or connected to bodily sensations?
  For example: a sensation being intensely present. Some discomfort or comfort. One small area asking for all your attention, or a larger area of the body. Different sensations, some subtle, others obvious. Prickling, tickling, or temperature changes. Please describe.

- Regarding the activity of your mind or the movement of thoughts?
  For example: thoughts moving faster or slowly. One idea, thought, or situation demanding your attention. Or were there many thoughts present, maybe scattered or jittery? Did you notice a shift in focus or attention? Did your quality of mind become clearer or more foggy? Please describe.

- In your emotions?
  For example: did you notice any emotion(s)? Did you notice any emotions arising and passing? Fading? Or

perhaps you became aware of the intensity of emotions becoming stronger or lighter? Please describe.

Remember, try not to analyse your answers or try to explain where sensations come from or why they are arising. Just notice what is present.

Make sure to read the *Wellbeing Prescription: Togetherness* in the final chapter of the book, where function, dosage, and precautions are elaborated.

PART II

Clarifying

Gather your insights:
Seeing yourself fully
and being brave

CHAPTER 4

Change
What changes you wish for, and why

As embodied beings alive in this web of existence, the only way to happiness is through conditioning our minds. Instead we are caught up in weaving the perception of our experiences into a belief of reality – this is what yogic philosophy calls the illusion, or maya. Each time we move through challenging times, we are confronted with maya, the illusion that hides reality from us. We can learn to see this as an opportunity to break free of our own conditioning and experience the world differently and with more truth.

Integration

In Part I: Normalizing, we examined the context of our lives – this day and age with its specific values, norms, and perspectives as they contribute to mental disorders, disease, or simply discomfort – and we spoke about how wisdom teachings like yoga, mindfulness, and compassion-based practices promote emotional wellbeing and can be useful when dealing with discomfort and worse. We discussed what Inner Spark is and found that it is in fact a part of us that is always present, though in challenging times it may become overshadowed. Now, in Part II: Clarifying, you're invited to inquire into yourself and hopefully bring new awareness into your current situation. In working towards clarification, you're taking the first steps towards disarming your struggle.

When we get caught up in our emotional struggles, we often fall into tunnel vision, which gives us only a very narrow and limited view of the situation we are in. From an evolutionary standpoint this is known as the scarcity principle. It is our normal and natural biological reaction to scarce resources and is triggered by our inner alarm system. The sympathetic activation of the nervous system is stimulated to ensure our engagement and focus is fully on the resources we're being deprived of. This is why we get stuck in looping, repetitive thoughts, ruminating over and over on one issue. It is simply our nervous system and the scarcity principle in full action mode, trying to help us attain that which we lack. Ruminating on one thing, we feel stuck, thinking only of what we cannot have, such as food, a relationship, more friends, more money, more ease, less stress, more time, and so on. There is truth in the saying 'what we fear, grows' and this is expressed through our neurotransmitters and in our nervous system, affecting our overall physical and psychological functioning. This feels like the exact opposite of the sense of flow that we want, the spontaneous positive immersion that Csikszentmihalyi described.

All we want is the body and mind to feel integrated, and a wholesome, easeful experience of being. We want the mind (that river of thoughts and the action of thinking) and our heart (meaning our emotions) to align and rest. We want how we feel about being alive, about ourselves, and about others and the world we live in to feel calm and comfortable. Yet we feel pain and think we see what is hurting us – we think we see what is to blame. Naturally we want out of the feelings brought about by dis-ease, by feeling disconnected or fragmented in body, mind, and heart. And then this yearning to feel aligned and connected, and to experience wholeness only intensifies the suffering.

As instructed in mindfulness-based meditations, we should always return to the body. To the here and now. To what is present and alive within you, in this moment. Always return to the body.

A patient, Peter, came to me seeking help for anxiety issues and panic attacks. He described himself as someone who had been anxious as a child, although he had not felt socially restricted by this. He had found strategies to deal with his anxious feelings and relied mostly on remaining close to a handful of childhood friends. As he grew into adulthood he turned to alcohol as a social lubricant. Though his use of alcohol never got out of hand, he felt he always needed a drink available to him at social engagements. He was a successful businessman when he found himself suddenly in the emergency room, at the age of twenty-eight, in fear that he was having a heart attack. After being fully examined by doctors, nothing was found, and the physician concluded that his heart arrhythmia, chest pain, and shortness of breath were stress-induced. She recommended that he make an appointment with a psychotherapist. When he showed up in my office, he had already had a number of panic attacks, and he had realized that these incidents were indeed anxiety attacks and not life-threatening in any way.

Panic attacks are obviously extremely uncomfortable. For those unfamiliar with such attacks, imagine feeling like your body is failing you, being terrified you might faint or even die. A panic attack is your body's alarm system caught in a severe round of the hiccups, and it just won't stop. It is signalling that you are in a situation of severe danger, although actually there is no danger at all. We could say that a panic attack shows that your built-in inner alarm system is working. The tricky part is that, once you've had an attack, you're likely to become fearful of having another one (whether this fear is conscious or unconscious, it is usually there). There is anxiety about potentially becoming anxious, and the fear that your body will once again fail you.

A common fear people then have is that this will happen where others can see you, and that this failing of body and mind to work in an integrated way will be clear to everyone around you. The fear is connected to a deep shame. The fear that others will think you have lost your mind can be paralysing. You worry people will think you have gone completely crazy and have no control over yourself.

These thoughts and the accompanying shame are poisonous and are paradoxically a relentless game our psyches play on us. The anxiety this creates holds us captive in the loop of the unnecessary activation of the inner alarm system.

Peter had realized that the incidents of extreme discomfort he was experiencing were indeed anxiety attacks, so when he came for treatment the biggest step had already been taken. However, it took him quite a while to accept that the attacks wouldn't just disappear. All he wanted was for his body to be on his side, to team up with the rest of him. As we began to uncover and clarify what was triggering the attacks, and to increase his awareness of how the symptoms expressed themselves, the anxiety became more familiar and more predictable. Little by little, the anxiety lost its panicky intensity, and with that its hold on him.

Did you know . . .

that practices such as deep breathing alleviate anxiety symptoms and can prevent relapse into attacks? They are safe and low-threshold interventions, and (while best learned from a certified teacher) they are easy and available for self-practice. The skills should be learned and cultivated when symptoms are not presenting (or when in remission). It is not recommended to focus your attention on inner sensations when anxiety is building. In addition to breathing practices (as referred to in Chapter 3), there are plenty of informal mindfulness practices that you can turn to when anxiety seems to creep up on you. You may want to take a mindful walk, or hit pause by giving your attention fully to your household chores instead of the ruminating mind, or you could choose to give mindful support and attention to someone else, and so forth. (See all eight Wellbeing Prescriptions in the final chapter.) The effects of these informal mindfulness practices can help you recognize when anxiety symptoms and the resulting pressure are on the rise, and strengthen your ability to not become overwhelmed by these symptoms. These practices help you see the nature of unease as a natural coming and going of sensations, despite the discomfort. It is recommended that mindfulness practices are integrated into your daily routine. In this way you will teach yourself to skilfully surf the waves of your symptoms.

. . . .

During periods of unease, it is difficult to see ourselves as integrated and whole or complete beings. We don't see clearly

and this is because we feel held back by external factors. 'If only this person could do that.' 'If only my situation were how I want it to be.' 'If only my life was different.' 'When I achieve this, then . . .' 'If only I didn't have so many bills.' 'If only I made more money . . .' And so on. We feel it is the external world that is responsible for the uncomfortable position we are in, and we'd like to let go. Don't we hear that a lot? Just let it go. A simple and oh-so-powerful release. Why don't you just let that shit go?! Well, although the act of letting go might seem simple, the really hard part is all the work before you can actually do it. We will look more in Chapter 6 at how to let go, but for now, it is important to acknowledge that while trying to let go you are likely to start judging yourself and this will bring you face to face with your inner critic. The veil of self-doubt, self-criticism, and feeling insecure is a heavy load to carry and it is an act of avoidance that won't serve you in the long run. You actually need the opposite, which in this case is integration.

In times of struggle we get caught in opposites: we may be scared of losing control, so we get entangled in over-controlling behaviour instead. Our focus is fully on what we don't want, and we are sure we want change but we have a hard time letting go of old habits. We want to be free but we try to take control of anything that could surprise us. It is one of the great paradoxes of being alive – we can be our best friend and our worst enemy all at once. We fail to see how our thinking actually keeps the struggle alive. And that is fine because, like I said earlier, being patient with yourself in times of intensity is the actual practice and it will prepare you to move on. It is easy to fall into self-criticism; self-blame and judgement are unfortunately often more easily awakened in us than understanding and acceptance. Being compassionate towards yourself and finding understanding for the fact that you do feel fragmented is hard. As is showing understanding for your inner struggles, seeing and acknowledging the difficult emotions present, and befriending your inner dark in that moment. These are truly difficult steps, but essential ones, and they will bring you closer to integration.

Even if you know you don't want to struggle, you probably don't know how to stop struggling. So let's start with what you do know. You know you want your life or your circumstances to be different. You may have clear ideas of what you desire for yourself, and you are likely to know very clearly what you don't want for yourself. This knowledge is actually a Nudge to Action. It suggests we take inventory. The aim of this next exercise is to describe yourself, as thoroughly as you can, with what is present in your life right now. Describe what contributes to any feelings you may have of being stuck, and what makes your life challenging right now. In this exercise, focus on what you don't want, and why.

Gain clarity: knowing what you don't *want*

A writing practice

Creating clarity for yourself is a way to bring yourself closer to the momentum of Inner Spark and integration. This step asks you to bring into awareness and acknowledge fully that which you actually wish to lean away from. You describe in your own words how your emotional struggles or feelings of unease have manifested in you and in your life right now. Before you can begin leaning in towards what you want, you need to be clear about what you wish to see changed. What is it that needs to be different in order for you to be happy?

In this process of gaining clarity through knowing what you don't want, I'm going to bring you into a writing meditation. I encourage you to describe this challenging time you are experiencing right now, as best as you can. To find clarity, you are asked to investigate the struggles you feel: how are they expressed in you, in body, mind, and heart? And how do they impact you in your daily life?

This exercise has three steps. Please set aside a minimum of 30–60 minutes. You need: a meditation cushion (or normal cushion), a blanket to cover yourself, a notebook, and a pencil.

Step 1: Silent contemplation

1. Find a comfortable seat somewhere where there are few distractions. Make sure your lower back, hips, and knees are supported.

2. You can close your eyes if you like or rest your gaze softly on the floor.

3. For the next 10 minutes, engage in contemplation by observing any phenomena of the mind, arising and passing in your attention. Whether it is a memory of the past, or a fantasy or worry about the future, or an idea or singular thought jumping around in the mind, simply observe what is present. Observe without analysing, changing, or removing anything from your attention. Trust that you are doing this correctly, observing the free-associative mind in this moment.

4. The aim of this exercise is to simply notice anything moving into the spotlight of your attention, to see it as it passes and then disappears, until something new demands your attention. There is no need to focus on anything in particular. Simply sit and notice what is moving within your mind.

5. To come out of this seated practice, take three deep breaths, inhaling deeply and exhaling fully, before gently opening your eyes and returning to the room.

Step 2: Spontaneous writing – what is it you don't want?

1. Sit comfortably with your notebook and pencil in front of you. Get ready to see on paper the

rollercoaster (or slow flow) of thoughts, emotions, and bodily sensations you find in yourself when in meditation. Prepare to meet and greet these inner sensations and emotions.

2. This exercise is an extension of your silent contemplation and is meant to connect you with the spontaneous flow of words that create your inner landscapes. As in the previous step, you observe the phenomena of mind arising into the spotlight of your attention. But this time you let the tip of your pencil be the spotlight, and allow whatever arises to pass through the pencil onto the paper.

3. Give yourself 15–30 minutes. Let the words pour onto the paper, directly connecting to the river of inner emotions.

4. Write down everything associated with the struggle or unease you are experiencing. Where does it hurt? What is the struggle? What are you unwilling to feel? Try answering questions like: what is it that I don't want present in my life right now? What is creating this struggle I feel? How does this struggle express itself in my daily life? How do I notice it? When is it mostly present? How does it interfere with my wellbeing? Does it affect my sleep or my appetite? Does it manifest as specific chains of thoughts? If so, try writing those out as specifically as possible. How does it make me feel? How long has it been like this?

5. When you're done, read through your writing. As you read, adopt an attitude of mindfulness. This means no judging, only absorbing and observing the words. Feel the sentiments that arise as you read.

6. Then summarize what you wrote by organizing your discoveries into the following phrases:

- When this or that happens . . . *or* When this person does that . . .

- It makes me think . . .

- It makes me feel . . .

- It expresses itself in my body as . . .

- It makes me (describe action or behaviour) . . .

Step 3: Logging out

1. Take 5 minutes to sit in silence once again. Give yourself a chance to log out of this exercise before returning to your everyday activities.

2. You can close your eyes if you want. What are you noticing right now? How do you feel? What is present in you after writing all this down? Notice what is present right now in your thoughts, your feelings, in your body. Sit with yourself in silence for a moment.

3. To come back, take a few deep breaths and return, opening your eyes when you feel ready.

Cultivating emotional tolerance

Now that you have more clarity on what you don't want in your life, it is time to discover what you do want. To fully understand what you want, however, you need to investigate how you embody and relate to those parts you don't desire.

You see, it is your attachment to these parts, and how they serve you (they have a function!), that informs you about how to take your next step. We tend to embody the dark parts or the parts of ourselves that we don't like in a specific way because they are part of our identity. They are part of the stories we tell ourselves about who we are. They serve a purpose as part of the illusion of who we think we are, in this embodied form. Therefore, the next step is to un-know what you think you know.

Typical thoughts or phrases in your storyline could be: 'The only thing I know is that it hurts so much.' Or: 'I know only one thing, and that is that I don't want my life to be like this.' Or: 'I really despise myself for thinking like this. For feeling like this. And that I keep feeling this way about myself, even if I don't want to. That I cannot lift my spirits.' So, you both acknowledge the struggle and at the same time you resist it. (Again, the paradox.) There is resistance to what you feel and to what is present within. This is not helpful, and it will not end the struggle you feel caught in. Trying to not feel what is actually there, or pretending it's not there, will only make the feelings worse. Instead, acknowledge fully what is there, and feel it – that is the true work you need to embark on. We'll look further into unravelling your storytelling mind in later chapters.

How we respond to our own emotional states and embody our feelings, especially the difficult ones and those that make us feel uneasy, is a key step towards understanding ourselves better and knowing where our resistance can be found. Think of feelings that cause a contracted sensation in the belly or a tightness in the chest, or the ones that make your shoulder and neck muscles harden and knot up. These are all bodily expressions of difficult feelings. Wisdom teachings and meditative practices build psychological resilience and emotional stamina and teach us to face our feelings with an equanimous mind, even when caught in the eye of the storm. This does not mean we are ignorant or avoidant. It means we stay present, we are understanding, and we remain balanced. We do not react with too much action or an attempt to control the situation; we neither withdraw nor avoid. Instead, we observe from a space of equanimity. When we do that the body may not tighten so much, the muscles needn't become knotted, and we remain calm and don't overreact.

Not that advanced meditators never yell in traffic (they do) or overreact in other ways, but when push comes to shove, they are able to draw on a quiet inner wisdom, and respond skilfully – and this is the key to unlocking their Inner Spark. As we know, the practices allow for neuroplasticity in the brain, especially in parts of the brain related to empathy and compassion and in the structures involved in taking informed decisions. We know, therefore, that we are capable of teaching ourselves new coping strategies. Meditative practices are skilful strategies and tools to be used to encourage and grow emotional wellbeing. What this means is that the more we practise – whether yoga or other more formal mindfulness-based practices – the more we train our capacity to respond to our own emotions. We learn to build in a buffer and become a witness. And over time we train our nervous system to rest more easily and more often and to cultivate resilience and tolerance. Our meditation practice stabilizes our baseline, our default mode, so that the alarm system is only activated when necessary.

Whether we find true equanimity will become clear only after many years of a dedicated meditation or yoga practice. Yet the short-term benefits are there too, and our practice can certainly help us along the way. We will become more curious about our own ways and less reactive, and with that hopefully also more compassionate and less judgemental. Skilfully accommodating our feelings and regulating our reactions are abilities we must learn and cultivate, as they help us build the resilience we need in times of struggle. They help us relate skilfully in the moment as difficult emotions arise, and help us embody those difficult emotions as they occur. These physical responses to emotions are neurobiological mechanisms, but we can still learn to self-regulate the intensity with which they present. This is true both for intense positive feelings and for intense negative feelings. Self-regulating and embodying these feelings means we steer ourselves away from avoidant behaviour or seeking out distractions that can be harmful to us and to our health.

In the end, to release ourselves from pain and struggle, this is exactly what we want to change: how emotions feel as we embody them. And we do this by being fully present in the body, by constantly investigating the body as it experiences emotions in the moment. This is an experience-based practice that teaches us how a thought or a feeling actually expresses itself through physical sensations in the body. And in this work of returning to the body, we find truth.

···

Did you know . . .

that emotional health and life mastery skills are on the agenda to become part of the elementary school curriculum in Norway as well as already being taught in UK schools? Hopefully this will help future generations view mental health from a more positive perspective. These developments are in line with

Aaron Antonovsky's work on salutogenesis, in which it is proven that focusing on activities that support wellbeing and health are beneficial (as opposed to pathogenesis, where the focus is on complaints and symptoms, so after illness has presented or when it is close to presenting). Both as a mother and as a psychologist, I find this wonderful news. I firmly believe our children should learn the basics surrounding mental and emotional health at an early age, just as they learn about physical health and exercise in their physical education classes.

Nina came to me because she believed she needed help with her eating habits and she felt uncomfortable in her body. In her early twenties, she was a resourceful student enrolled in higher education, and while her friends were having fun, she was suffering emotionally. And she wasn't really eating, she confessed. Realizing she needed to take her health seriously, she had started taking yoga classes. However, she had chosen Ashtanga Vinyasa yoga, and this six-days-a-week strict style of practice was actually triggering her already overreactive perfectionist personality, rather than giving her the promised sense of ease and relaxation. Similarly, she was convinced that her mostly vegan diet was the healthiest way to approach food. In reality, however, this diet became the perfect way for her to legitimize her restrictive eating habits and continue her disordered eating behaviours. She had struggled with eating habits for years, starting when she felt out of shape in her teens and was bullied, and continuing during her parents' divorce. She had gone through years of difficulty with no way of carefully embodying her emotions. During the year before she came to see me, she had been living by herself, excelling at university, and for the first time had a feeling of control over her life. That feeling of control was, however, an illusion. In an unsuccessful attempt to control her inner chaos and the flood of emotions overwhelming her system, she had started to become over-controlling, from her study patterns to her yoga to her eating habits. Every day was rigorously planned and controlled.

As our therapeutic work proceeded, it became clear to her that she was afraid to embody the dormant emotions that lay hiding within her. The feelings she had hidden deep inside after being bullied, excluded by her peers, and battered by harsh words raining down on her, had to surface. As did the immense pain lingering in her belly since the day her parents had sat her and her brother down and told them they were going to separate. She watched her world fall apart, but she kept it together – at least to the outside world – to protect her parents. She didn't want to be another burden for them to deal with during their break-up. To accommodate this, she became the queen of helping others, delivering the best possible results in whatever was asked of her and always hiding her emotions, and paying the price for that with her own deteriorating health. However, this strategy was now beginning to fail her. She began having emotional outbursts at odd moments: crying in the middle of a lecture, or raging at someone who cleaned up her stuff for her. Her social life was more or less non-existent as any meal-related occasion was off limits for her. And to make things even worse, her grades started to drop. She was unable to perform because the only thing she could think about was food. She was hungry as hell. What she was doing was not serving her and she wanted change. She longed for a happier and more balanced life; she longed to feel good, healthy, and in touch with herself. Even though she was not sure she wanted to give up her restrictions on food, she was sure that she wanted a change. Most importantly, she knew that life had more to offer her than what she was giving herself and she wanted to experience that. She wanted to enjoy life, to relax and laugh. She wanted in on the fun parts. With this to motivate her, we embarked on the difficult task of looking deeply into the events, the relationships, and situations that had imprisoned her, and we discovered the inner storyteller that had caused her pain. Simultaneously we found behaviours and thoughts she was willing to exchange for more constructive ones.

There are no shortcuts in recovering from an eating disorder, and the process is a long one. Each case is unique, and when and whether intervention might be helpful should be individually assessed. I recommend multidisciplinary treatments. Please connect with your doctor for information on the best treatment facilities in your area.

. . . .

Did you know . . .

that our proximity to nature might affect our mental health more than we think, and can predict how we will feel in the future too? With urbanization on the rise, we have seen a parallel increase in mental health issues. And we know that living in densely populated areas paradoxically creates heightened feelings of loneliness. We also know that living in close proximity to nature decreases aggression and attention-deficit issues, and increases health and social functioning. These are all key ingredients found in a state of ease and wellbeing. Connecting to nature revitalizes our overall psychological functioning. The Attention Restoration Theory (ART) argues that nature plays a valuable role in overcoming mental fatigue and shows how nature heals and calms us, which in turn enables us to handle conflicts and social relationships better. ART studies show that close proximity to nature is even linked to lower levels of criminality. In addition nature increases our attention span and thus increases our ability to concentrate. This is interesting because cognitive lapses such as reduced attention are seen in most cases of mental health deterioration. This gives us some strong and solid reasons to spend more time in nature or connecting to nature (house plants or trees in the middle of a city are nature too) as a prevention and recovery tool when dealing with emotional disease and as a part of treatment for mental health disease.

Our threefold brain

After looking into our inner nature and how we can strengthen emotional tolerance to build resilience and learn to experience our emotions with equanimity, and touching on the whole of nature's effect on our wellbeing, it is time to look more deeply into the mechanics of the brain. Understanding how the major pathways of brain communication flow, especially in relation to our inner alarm system, can help us become gentler towards ourselves.

The human brain is fascinating. To start with, our brain is not actually one brain but three! The threefold brain consists of what we refer to as the reptilian brain, the limbic brain, and the neocortex. The reptilian brain is located where the spine meets the skull and is the doorway through which major sensory information first passes. This part of the brain regulates the homeostatic systems and vital organs. Think of heart rate, breathing pace, temperature, sleep, appetite, and the experience of safety and danger. It operates at the instinctual level, meaning it is rather compulsive and rigid, and it speaks a beautiful yet subtle language of bodily sensations. These sensations are experienced in three ways: *exteroception* – the sensitivity to stimuli outside of the body; *interoception* – the awareness or sensitivity to stimuli inside of the body; and *proprioception* – the unconscious perception of movement and spatial orientation arising from stimuli within the body. Research has shown that clinically depressed conditions lead to a muted sense of body awareness and a reduced sensitivity to interoception.

The limbic brain refers to the structures that emerged in the first mammals. It is located deeper in the centre of the brain, almost at the brain's core. It is commonly known as the 'emotional seat' and is involved in motivation, emotions, learning, and behaviour. This is where value judgements are born and where the scarcity principle is regulated. These structures are responsible for the decisions we make regarding our relationships and how we interact. The limbic brain is the home of emotional and social engagement.

The neocortex is the outermost layer of the cerebral cortex in a humanoid brain. We usually speak about this referring to the prefrontal cortex, which is located in the forehead. The neocortex is responsible for higher brain functions such as sensory perception and the generation of motor commands, and the intellectual qualities of our being such as cognition, language, abstract thinking and logic, and how to move from insights to action. The language of this part is verbal. Psychotherapy typically addresses the neocortex and (depending on which approach is used) the limbic brain, and aspects of relationships and memory are included as part of the therapeutic process. Mindfulness and compassion-based practices of Eastern wisdom teachings work with the language not only of the neocortex but also of the limbic brain (emotions) and the reptilian brain (bodily sensations). This is one of the reasons why these practices and mindful yoga and breath work are beneficial when incorporated in mental health treatment plans. They awaken body awareness, emotional presence, and cognition all at once, speaking to all three parts of the brain simultaneously. The approach is one of integration of all parts and becomes a holistic experience.

The communication between our three brains and the body is regulated by the nervous system. The autonomic nervous system is in charge of unconscious behaviours, such as regulating bodily functions that our minds don't control. This nervous system consists of two major parts: the sympathetic and the parasympathetic pathways. The sympathetic is connected to activating our alertness and, if needed, the fight-or-flight mode. The parasympathetic system is our at-ease mode and is connected to the vagus nerve – the brakes for the fight-or-flight mode. When the vagus nerve is balanced and toned, we experience a state of ease as there is a healthy connection between the limbic brain and the neocortex. This allows us to engage in emotional and social interactions in healthy ways and to make decisions skilfully. If a potential danger is perceived, the sympathetic nervous system can override this by releasing neurochemicals that will lead to a higher state of alertness. When this happens, communication between the limbic system and the neocortex is cut off, or given little to no power, and survival is prioritized. If the situation is too dangerous for even fight-or-flight, the vagus nerve may override these reactions and activate a freeze response through the reptilian brain. This is often reported as a response by trauma survivors.

Remember Peter who suffered from panic attacks? You can now see that his sympathetic nervous system was in a state of hyperarousal, even though there was no actual life-threatening danger, and that this disabled smooth communication to the neocortex. The tone of the vagus nerve is low when people suffer from anxiety, and he was therefore not able to find his way back into a state of ease. He used alcohol to self-medicate and this gave him temporary relief from the heightened activation of the sympathetic system. This illustrates how it can benefit us to learn about the pathways and activations of the nervous system, and how this knowledge, when combined with yogic breathing techniques and with psychotherapeutic work, can help us find relief from conditions related to anxiety. Connecting all three parts of the brain is actually a way to empower yourself.

Information flows between all three brains, and the quality of the communication depends on the health of the pathways. The quality of these pathways can be improved thanks to neuroplasticity – the fact that our brains have the ability to continuously develop, change, and restructure. But if the neural pathways are not worked or stimulated, they will lose their strength. These communication pathways can even become weaker so that communication between the three brains diminishes severely. And they can also be strengthened – through yoga, mindfulness, and compassion-based practices that build emotional stamina and allow us to experience ease more readily. How open the pathways are is decisive in how easily we move from being in a reactive mode to responding more skilfully and with awareness, and perhaps even with more equanimity. The bottom line is that, for effortless communication between all three brain parts, we need a well-toned vagus nerve. In states of unease, when communication between the brain parts is not as smooth and access to the neocortex is down, the tone of the vagus nerve is weak.

A well-toned vagus nerve is directly connected to what mindfulness-based practices understand as a healthy response mode (as opposed to the autopilot mode that lacks awareness) and results in a strong autonomic nervous system in which the prefrontal cortex is engaged, allowing for an adequate, calm response to stressors. Meditative practices are excellent ways to strengthen this connection, to tone the vagus nerve, and to keep the nervous system attuned and well regulated. As you engage in meditative practices while in your at-ease mode, it becomes easier to find the brakes on your stress response in challenging times, making you more tolerant towards outside stimuli.

Understanding the underlying psychology and neuro-biology of how we respond to change can support you in being more compassionate towards yourself when you go through difficult times. Remember that you need a little time to strengthen that vagus nerve and to recalibrate your nervous system. You will get there.

Now it is time for the next Nudge to Action: getting to know what you want more of in your life.

Gain clarity: knowing what you do want

A writing practice

This exercise is the next step in your process towards step-ping out of emotional struggle and towards creating clarity and moving closer to the momentum of your Inner Spark. In the previous exercise, you inventoried what you didn't want in your life. Now you are invited to figure out what it is you *do* want in your life. What do you want to keep, or what do you believe might serve you better now? And how do you want to see your life and your circumstances, right now? This exercise requires some bravery and courage. Think of courage as it comes from the French word *coeur* (heart), and realize you want to be fully honest with yourself now because you are about to start taking some decisions. Don't worry, at first these decisions are only on paper. And I will guide you through them as you describe as elaborately as you can what it is that you wish to see more of in your life.

As in the previous exercise, this one also has three steps. Please set aside a minimum of 30–60 minutes. You need: a meditation cushion (or normal cushion), a blanket to cover yourself, a notebook, and a pencil.

Step 1: Silent contemplation

1. Find a comfortable seat somewhere where there are few distractions. Make sure your lower back, hips, and knees are supported.

2. You can close your eyes if you like or rest your gaze softly on the floor.

3. For the next 10 minutes, engage in contemplation by observing any phenomena of the mind, arising and passing in your attention. Whether it is a memory of the past, or a fantasy or worry about the future, or an idea or singular thought jumping around in the mind, simply observe what is present. Observe without analysing, changing, or removing anything from your attention. Trust that you are doing this correctly, observing the free-associative mind in this moment.

4. The aim of this exercise is to simply notice anything moving into the spotlight of your attention, to see it as it passes and then disappear, until something new demands your attention. There is no need to focus on anything in particular. Simply sit and notice what is moving within your mind.

5. To come out of this seated practice, take three deep breaths, inhaling deeply and exhaling fully, before gently opening your eyes and returning to the room.

Step 2: Spontaneous writing – what you wish for

1. Sit comfortably with your notebook and pencil in front of you. Get ready to see appear on paper the rollercoaster (or slow flow) of thoughts, emotions, and bodily sensations you find in yourself when in meditation. Prepare to meet and greet your innermost thoughts.

2.	This exercise is an extension of your silent contemplation and is meant to connect you with the spontaneous flow of words that create your inner landscapes. As in the previous step, you observe the phenomena of mind arising into the spotlight of your attention. But this time you let the tip of your pencil be the spotlight and allow whatever arises to pass through the pencil onto the paper.

3.	Give yourself 15–30 minutes. Let the words pour onto the paper, directly connecting to the river of inner emotions.

4.	Write out everything associated with how you want to feel. Try answering questions like: what is it that I want present in my life right now? Try writing without feeling inhibited by practicalities, and instead describe what you want as elaborately as you can, as if anything is possible. Do you wish for more time? What do you wish to use this time for? Do you wish for more stability in your financial situation? How would this bring more ease into your life? Do you wish for better health? In what way? And how would you like to get there? Do you wish for more positive thinking? Write everything out as specifically as possible.

5.	When you're done, read through your writing. As you read, adopt an attitude of mindfulness. This means no judging, only absorbing and observing the words. Feel the sentiments that arise as you read.

6.	Then summarize what you wrote by organizing your discoveries into the following phrases:

- For me to feel more at ease, I wish for . . .

- For me to feel more at ease, I wish for . . .

- For me to feel more at ease, I wish for . . .

Step 3: Logging out

1. Take 5 minutes to sit in silence once again. Give yourself a chance to log out of this exercise before returning to your everyday activities.

2. You can close your eyes if you want. What do you notice right now? How do you feel? What is present in you after writing all this down? Notice what is present right now in your thoughts, in your feelings, in your body. Sit with yourself in silence for a moment.

3. To come back, take a few deep breaths and return, opening your eyes when you feel ready.

Make sure to read the *Wellbeing Prescription: Nature* in the final chapter of the book, where function, dosage, and precautions are elaborated.

CHAPTER 5

Radical Freedom
The function of conditioning

*In the land of snow-drizzled mountains you are held in
a winter embrace of beautiful darkness. This is a time for
you to hibernate and fully embody your inner landscapes.
In this space of embodiment you will find that you are the
agent of your own light, the one igniting your Inner Spark
and finding your purpose. Like stardust and atoms find their
spark from within, so do you. Knowingly or unknowingly,
just know that you sparkle.*

Obstacles to overcome

Why is it so difficult to step out of struggle? What is holding
you back from the change you want? How do you usually
react to your inner unease? What do you do to maintain a
feeling of control when the inner chaos feels too intense? Do
you reach for food or alcohol? Aggression? Self-harm? What
do you need to be able to move towards what you wish for in
your life?

After deepening our understanding of the threefold brain
and how this relates to emotional stability and equanimity,
and putting into words what you don't want and what you do
want in your life in the previous chapter, the next important

step is discerning which obstacles you need to overcome in order to step out of the struggle. Also it is a good idea to evaluate whether you have at your disposal the tools needed to overcome these obstacles so that you can move towards what you want.

As we saw in the first part of this book, we tend to hold ourselves captive in our status quo even if it doesn't serve us. Our current state is what we know and is familiar to us, what feels normal. So we stick to it and it confirms how we perceive ourselves and our core beliefs regarding our place in this world. That which is predictable is comfortable and helps us anticipate how we will respond to the stressors we are exposed to.

However, if you are to move towards the life you want, you need to lean in actively towards the change you wish to see in your life and in yourself. You need to investigate what will move you from wishing towards acting. For example, perhaps you have stated that you don't want to feel lonely any more. Or that you don't want to feel overwhelmed by negative inner dialogue, that you'd like to be kinder to yourself in difficult times. Or that you wish to be happier and to have more fun. What do you need to do to make this happen? What are the obstacles you need to overcome within yourself? I realize that's easier said than done, so let's unravel what hinders you in moving towards this change that you desire.

Conditioning of mind, obstacles to agency

The main obstacles are usually rooted in the core beliefs we hold that are a result of our conditioning and upbringing. These conditionings and core beliefs are the blueprints of our nature and of how we were nurtured. Conditioning is what we have learned about how reality unfolds, as well as about our place in this world and where we fit in. Your conditioning is a set of mental constructions integrated into your belief system. They are the building blocks of your core beliefs that are expressed in thoughts and feelings. This is all the result of what is shown to us by our parents or caregivers through their behaviours, ways of thinking, and how they deal with their emotions. Naturally this is all also a result of their own conditioning and it is dependent on their own parents or caregivers. Our conditioning can thus be seen as hereditary and transferred from generation to generation.

Potential obstacles are always present in us in various ways and at various times in our lives. Some obstacles result from the situation or life phase that we are in, some are genetic (like addictions), and some are deeply embedded emotional wounds resulting from complex and traumatizing interpersonal exchanges (with parents and/or caregivers or others). These wounds may also be the result of neglect by our parents or caregivers. As you may remember from the 'quality of being' model in Chapter 3, when we are in a state of unease, skilful action is inhibited and this gives us the feeling of being stuck. This further inhibits communication between the three brains and their pathways, and decreases vagus nerve toning. Let's take a closer look at these obstacles, and find clarity regarding which obstacles are present for you now, and how they serve you. Remember, to be free you need to see what has a hold on you.

There's a duality we cannot ignore when dealing with this subject matter. On the one hand, we need the nurturing attachments of relationships – of being seen, heard, and understood – but on the other hand we also need to find and feel our independence.

The following obstacles are in no particular order and they often overlap.

Obstacles to freedom

Reward junkies, moving from intention

We are pleasure seekers and dopamine junkies and we love getting what we want. I remember becoming aware of these thoughts and cravings as a teenager: 'If I have this or that, then I will feel great.' Thoughts like this illustrate the mind's ability to create future goals in order to motivate our actions. We set a goal and, depending our state of mind, the work we then do to achieve that goal becomes either an experience of flow or a desperate and rigid ride to disappointment. Our habit is to set a goal, expect a specific outcome that we can predict, and when we get it our brains reward us with a shot of dopamine. And we feel great! Until the dopamine wears off. Then the next thing we want becomes a desire and a goal and our mission . . . This is how we become hooked, and before we know it we have become reward junkies.

Don't get me wrong, it is not bad that we are able to set goals and pursue them. In fact, this is one of the qualities that sets us apart as a species. It is just that our attitudes as we work towards our goals, and the way we relate to the goal, so often tend to cause us trouble. If we are too attached to the outcome, we believe there is only one way out of our situation. This type of tunnel vision is the opposite of mindfulness, and creates a tightness and a holding. It creates stress. Working towards our goals while being mindful – observing whatever arises and passes in our attention, with kindness and curiosity – is a gentler way to move towards our goals. We don't lose sight of the bigger picture and we can work with a broader perspective.

My client Liza came to me because she was falling into a depression. She recognized the symptoms as she had experienced this fairly regularly since her early teens. As we worked on empowering her and moving towards more wellbeing, it became clear that what she feared most was being lonely. She held core beliefs, based on childhood experiences, that she didn't fit in or was being left out, and these beliefs had become the guiding narrative of her inner voice: 'I don't belong with anyone. I will always be alone.' Liza had been involved in a very irregular, on-and-off relationship for two years when she first came to see me. She was determined to remain in the relationship even though the man she was dating had made it very clear he was not interested in any form of commitment to her. Liza's biggest wish, on the other hand, was to get married and take the relationship to the next level. Their relationship goals couldn't have been further apart on the spectrum, yet she was not considering leaving the relationship since she did not want to be alone. Liza's behaviour was proving that she would rather stay in a non-committed relationship, on someone else's terms, than create space to meet someone who was willing to commit.

Each time her partner confirmed that he didn't want to take their relationship to the next level, Liza fell into a vicious circle of ruminating thoughts and ended up feeling hopelessly paralysed by the whole situation. She wanted something else for herself and for her life, but she wasn't able to act. The fear of being alone had her tightly in its grip. There was a deeper wound in Liza that needed to heal. She had been focusing on wanting a committed relationship, but not on the wound she needed to take care of. Shifting her attention from the desperate need to be in a relationship to the fear of being alone was a huge step for her. She started to see where her behaviour was coming from and that it was an expression of her core beliefs. We focused on what behaviours would be more suitable for her and how she could shift her attention towards confirming she wasn't alone in this world. Of course, depressions are very complex, but this example shows how a desperate desire for a certain outcome (relationship/marriage) can become an obstacle and hide the actual issue (fear of being alone/core belief of not fitting in).

At first Liza couldn't see the real obstacle standing in the way of her happiness as she was too focused on being in a relationship. But when she was ready, she learned to direct her focus and efforts towards a way that could serve her better. When she saw her fear of loneliness was motivating her actions, she turned her attention to the wound in herself. She began to see it, understand where it came from, and she began to nurture and care for herself. She found this commitment to herself empowering, and learned to work her way through behavioural patterns and ways of thinking that made her feel alone, instead of focusing on being with someone who wasn't committing to her. Committing to yourself (like Liza did), and to the process rather than the outcome, could actually be the very strategy you need to step out of your struggle.

Remind yourself how this journey towards Inner Spark began: with you setting an intention of kindness for yourself and committing to being patient with yourself. When we set intentions and focus on what is present and the resources we have to move towards healing, we tune into what is possible with an equanimous calm mind and we can see the potential of what may come. It's a matter of living in the present, instead of worrying or trying to control a future outcome.

Defence mechanisms, setting boundaries

Unless we are aware of them, protecting our core beliefs or defending the way we've been conditioned happens mostly on autopilot. Our core beliefs are embedded in us when we are young children crawling deep into the comfort of the rabbit's fur. We create our nests of normality and adopt behaviours that match and continuously confirm our beliefs. And although it is essential we develop autonomy and a sense of self, when we struggle we are often faced with how viciously we protect this sense of self. Think about what you do when you are faced with challenges. What behaviours do you fall into? What do you do to soothe yourself or to avoid feeling the discomfort that comes with the struggle? Do you self-medicate? Turn to people? Sex? Food? Spiritual explanations? Drugs? Restrictions? Rigidity? How far do you go to protect your core beliefs? How far do you go in order to avoid feeling those difficult feelings?

Storm, a young man in his mid-twenties, wanted to meet new people. And most of all he hoped to meet that special someone. He had a few friends, but he didn't consider them to be very close friends. His social anxiety hindered him greatly in trying new things and going out. He feared that if he talked to someone new they would quickly discover that he was as boring and as strange as he firmly believed himself to be. As far as I could tell from our therapeutic relationship, he was neither boring nor strange. He was sweet, considerate, and empathetic. Yet he was falling into social isolation by protecting his core belief that he was boring and strange. He didn't want anyone to see how uncomfortable he became when trying to connect with others. We worked patiently and steadily and found a way for him to negotiate with himself. He found a desire within himself to let go of those behaviours and the accompanying beliefs, but really letting go felt like a huge jump off the rabbit's fur into the unknown. We had to find alternative strategies that he felt he could trust as he began to move into the unknown, outside the rabbit's fur. He decided to seek out a group activity or situation where he could go and meet others casually, like a group training session, a hiking group, or something similar. He wanted to step out of his comfort zone and engage with others but within certain boundaries. He needed to be able to prepare himself for meeting people: 'Hi, my name is Storm. I'm new in this group. What's your name? Have you been here before? What made you sign up for this?' We took the necessary time to prepare Storm, and the first time he went to such an occasion he enjoyed a positive experience. He realized that he had managed himself well – and, with that, the biggest obstacle had been overcome.

So how do we shift our behaviour from these defence mechanisms and avoidance patterns to more useful behaviour? How can we start seeing them as patterns and not as ourselves or our personalities? Can we lean away from these deeply ingrained habits and beliefs? Changing our ways means doing things differently so that we can be in the world differently and experience ourselves differently. These are huge steps. When overcoming obstacles like Storm did and trying new things, clear boundaries and clear steps are essential. Storm needed courage and support in this process, but it was the boundaries that made him feel safe enough to eventually make the move. Step by step he began to move through his struggle. It can be frightening to give up a pattern that no longer serves you. The clear steps keep your inner alarm system turned off or just slightly on alert.

. . . .

Did you know . . .
that yoga erases the habitual patterns of the mind? By continuously committing to seeing yourself within a larger framework, and finding insight about and within yourself, yoga becomes a stepping stone to radical freedom – freedom from the patterns of your mind.

. . . .

The downward spiral, doing things differently

Low energy is a major hindrance in moving forward. It imprisons us and holds us hostage in a void. Low energy can have many reasons and causes, but when a lack of energy persists over time, depressive symptoms will begin to manifest. Inertia takes us into a downward spiral and can lock us in till we feel stuck in our bodies and in our thoughts.

Stella had turned her life around some years ago. After experiencing burnout, she had embarked on a major career change and had become a yoga teacher. She had found joy starting afresh and had been enjoying her new life and work. But when she came to see me, she had been struggling for a while. A knee injury some six months earlier had put her on the bench. She couldn't work much and needed to rest in order to heal. This downtime had led her to discover various ambiguous symptoms in her body. Soon she was in and out of hospitals and doctor's appointments, getting her heart, belly, and abdomen checked. Nothing was found. But Stella was convinced there was something very wrong with her and she felt sure it was something physical. She self-diagnosed herself according to Ayurvedic principles that she had learned in yoga training, and changed her diet accordingly. She did all of this from the belief there was something wrong with her. None of her interventions helped and nothing put her mind at ease either. They did, however, help her uphold her core belief that there was something wrong. By dealing with her symptoms, she felt she could exert some scope of control over her sense of inertia. But all the health interventions she was putting herself through failed to acknowledge the downward spiral of thought that she was stuck in. She was ignoring the voice in her head that was saying: 'You will not succeed, you are not important. A yogic lifestyle is the best remedy. That you are not healthy confirms there is something very wrong with you. You are not doing it right, you are not good enough.'

Stella felt hopeless. She believed her situation was caused by external powers, by something she wasn't able to exercise any control over. Her knee injury had caused her to be less active, and now she felt tired, she was sleeping more, and there weren't many opportunities for her to work. She struggled as feelings of meaninglessness began to creep up on her. Her income was plummeting, and this caused despair. Doctors couldn't find anything wrong with her, which only added to her despair. She wanted them to fix it, fix her. But there was nothing to fix. Stella's example illustrates that it is not only *what* we do but *how* we do it that informs our state of being. Sometimes we need to take a closer look at how we deal with our situation, how we perceive it, and see how we can take action in more skilful ways. We may find we need to do things very differently in order to set ourselves free.

Unease and building tolerance

We touched upon unease and emotional tolerance in previous chapters, and I'd like to further clarify how unease typically expresses itself. Unease is a commonly used term that describes quite generally what struggle feels like. In fact, unease refers to a wide range of emotions and feelings such as anxiousness, worrying, various bodily expressions of emotional stress, emotional turbulence, interpersonal conflicts causing tension, symptoms of stress, or restlessness. Restlessness is the most common description given when people are asked to describe their uneasiness. They speak of an inner restlessness not only in the body but also in the mind. When pressed further, they describe ruminating thoughts and intense emotions plaguing them.

What is this restlessness really? We've all experienced ruminating thoughts at some point in our lives. It is the monkey mind stepping up its acrobatic antics when the going gets a little tough. It's all that thinking that you do, thinking again and again about the same little thing . . . and overthinking. It is when you're trying to think your way out of your struggle. Going inwards, deeper and deeper, looking for the answers to free yourself from feeling so stuck. But you don't find your answers in your thoughts. So not only does the monkey mind not free you, but it creates a feeling of restlessness that actually makes the situation you're in feel even more frustrating. All you find in the monkey mind is more thinking: chains of thought that take you hostage, focusing on concerns and worries. Then soon enough anxiousness presents. And you are stuck. The downward spiral has manifested itself.

Lilly had come to therapy after some hesitation. She admitted she felt ambivalent about this decision, but she wanted help with the inertia and low energy she was experiencing. She felt trapped and unable to connect to an inner source of energy; she felt lethargic and stuck. She had quit her job as it had failed to inspire her and she didn't want to work somewhere where she felt she wasn't contributing to the best of her ability. But now she lacked the energy she needed to find another job. Any job she read about seemed wrong. And her worries about money, bills, her rent, and her health were beginning to consume her. She described her situation as feeling paralysed, trapped in her own skin. I asked her: 'Where in your body do you notice this feeling of entrapment?' She paused and stared down into her lap, her arms tightly wrapped around her as if to hold herself together. 'I don't know,' she started. 'I'm not sure . . . What do you mean by "where in my body"? I just feel all these thoughts, jumping around. From when I open my eyes in the morning, until I fall asleep somewhere in the middle of the night, consumed by anxiety.' Her body was not part of her narrative. She didn't feel there was much of a connection. Later she revealed that she felt shame about her body and that for years she had wished her body had been different. Since her connection to her body was so poor, she was unable to decipher signals from her body or to detect emotional expressions in her body.

- -

Did you know ...
that body awareness increases with practices such as mindful yoga? Body awareness – or the kinaesthetic or felt sense of the body – increases the ability to differentiate more accurately between thoughts, bodily sensations, and emotions. This is highly beneficial for those hoping to build emotional tolerance.

- -

Doubt and hope

When we feel stuck and when we struggle to control difficult emotions moving in our inner landscapes, things can feel overwhelming. And when we feel overwhelmed and unable to skilfully regulate these intense emotions, doubt and self-doubt loom around the corner. We begin to doubt we'll find our way out of these dark times and we lose faith things will improve. We lose hope. We may even start thinking there's something fundamentally wrong with us, that we really cannot change our lives or ourselves. We doubt we have the skills required to shift towards the life we want. This is, of course, not true. But it is important to acknowledge and see the hold that doubt has on you, and the lack of hope that you are going through. How do these express themselves, and why? We do this so we can breathe some life back into hope. We must do this because feeling hope is an essential catalyst towards emotional wellbeing and towards integrated health.

. . . .

Did you know ...

that hope has an impact on our emotional wellbeing? In the book *The Science of Optimism and Hope: Research essays in honor of Martin E.P. Seligman* (2000), a chapter by C.R. Snyder on the Hope Mandala concludes that people who have high hopes are obviously faced with challenges just as much as those with lower hopes. But the difference is that high-hopers are better able to cope when dealing with obstacles, and their overall feelings of wellbeing are higher. People with high hopes feel less overwhelmed by emotional challenges and have easier access to inner agency in difficult times. Snyder appreciates the cyclic movement of our inner landscapes in a beautiful way when he says: 'There is an ebb and flow to hopeful thinking.'

. . . .

When we face a crisis, we can lose the hope that there is kindness in the world, and this is a particularly dire state to be in. This may happen during significant life events like losing a job, being made redundant, during severe illness, or losing someone we love. This could also happen when we embody a new role or phase in our lives, such as when transitioning from childhood and becoming a teenager, becoming a husband or a wife, becoming a parent, or seeing yourself become a caretaker to a parent. This is actually all part of the dance of life. We can expect the presence of doubt and the wavering of hope to be part of what we go through. And they can help us eventually find more faith. As we develop faith in ourselves, in the world, in the greater good and more, we become empowered.

Having hope is not the same as expecting a certain outcome. Having hope is simply trusting that things will work themselves out, somehow. The state of inertia you are stuck in will pass. Just like everything else in this world, this particular situation is an arising and passing moment. The well-known author and researcher Daniel Goleman writes that a sense of hope is a predictor of agency and can also say something about how motivated you are to change. It is important that hope is not confused with expectation. Expectation leans on desire and the wish for a particular outcome. Hope leans on one's own abilities to access agency in times of struggle.

Feeling hopeful in difficult times is easier said than done. That's why social support and relationships are so important. Reach out for support and help if needed, for example through mentorship, therapy, or spiritual advisors. If you find yourself in doubt or without hope for improvement, then ask for help. And do so sooner rather than later because, as the pain and discomfort builds, it becomes increasingly difficult to ask for help. Use your sense of hope as a guiding light for what kind of support you need right now. Don't judge yourself or condemn how you feel. If hope feels far off, acknowledge that, embrace it, but do ask for help.

The function of the obstacles

We've looked into some of the obstacles that stand in the way of change and the underlying mechanisms that obstruct us in taking any initiatives towards change. It is important to acknowledge the presence of these hindrances in daily life, because when we see them, we can also see why they are there. We then often find that they serve a purpose. Like bubble wrap around a glass vase, they have an important function: they act as a defence mechanism to protect our core beliefs. These obstacles to change defend our beliefs against anything (or anyone) who questions them.

For this reason, we attempt to the best of our abilities to organize our lives and the people we expose ourselves to in accordance with the often-subconscious core beliefs we have about ourselves. These beliefs are a result of our conditioning, the knowledge and thought patterns we hold as a result of interacting with our surroundings, in particular with our parents and caregivers, since we were born. In yogic philosophy this is known as *maya*, or the illusion of reality. We understand perceived information as the truth, while it is actually an illusion. Buddhist philosophy calls this *samsara*, the existence we are caught up in in the material world. And the only way to liberate ourselves from the illusion is to drop all patterns. Then, nirvana is achievable. Yogis called this *moksha*, freedom from *maya*. If you want to live a better life in the here and now, it is important you understand radical freedom as knowing yourself well, and knowing your patterns too, so you are able to respond to emotions skilfully and understand others more compassionately, interacting with others with integrity – for the benefit of all.

Now, whether you drink a few glasses of wine daily to relax because you're so stressed, restrict what you eat in an attempt to control difficult emotions, or isolate yourself at home out of fear of having a panic attack in front of others, it is safe to say our behaviour always has a function. Usually seemingly destructive behaviour is a defence mechanism in action serving a purpose. Behaviour that may seem off–key to an outsider is often an attempt to deal with difficult emotional situations that are intense, uncomfortable, or even over-whelming. In order to liberate yourself from the emotional struggle, you need to acknowledge what the behavioural obstacles standing in your way are and also how they serve you, and then you need to find other more constructive and skilful means to support you in the process of change.

Fortunately our brains are wired to change, and neuroplasticity is ongoing throughout our lives. Continuous practice is therefore essential if we want our brain structure to change as we work towards changing our ways and creating new habits. For example, when we practise mindfulness, we actually practise an attitude of non-judgemental loving kindness and holding the attention in the here and now, and we get better at it over time as we sit in silence, observing the rising of thoughts and the passing of them. We don't get better at meditating, we get better at finding this calm mental space. The more we sit to practise this, the easier it is to get into the 'meditative attitude'. We may not feel much better at calming our minds, and it's unlikely we have fewer thoughts, but the observing of the mind or the thoughts – the meta perspective – becomes more easily accessible to us. We learn to take heed of our own mind.

For example, you might begin to observe as follows: 'I have an intense emotion connected to this memory of that conversation I had with my brother last year.' Or: 'I'm noticing bodily sensations in this moment that feel uncomfortable. I notice feelings of anger and fear. There is also sadness. And I'm thinking about that argument I had last week with my partner.'

When we have taken these steps to clarify what is

happening within us, we become ready to take action. And in doing so, the knowledge that we can actually change is a great comfort. We can practise whatever new behaviour or way of thinking we want again and again, until it becomes internalized and integrated into our way of being. Like the late Sri Pattabhi Jois would remind his students of Ashtanga Vinyasa yoga: 'Practise, practise, practise, and all is coming.' As long as you continue practising diligently, he was saying, you'll integrate the underlying philosophy of yoga into your mind, deconstructing the old conditionings and core beliefs you have about the world and yourself, and creating new and strong ones.

With this in mind, let's take a closer look at the barriers in our minds that keep us from stepping into change fully, and discover how to get rid of them. Because even though I make change sound easy ('just practise'), I realize there are obstacles that we need to deal with. And in Chapter 6 we'll look concretely at ambivalence and evaluate your readiness for change.

Radical freedom

The process of radically freeing yourself from the conditionings of your mind and your core beliefs takes courage, willingness, commitment, patience, action, and compassion. It's easy to fall into self-criticism and judgement. As we saw in Chapter 2, our generation has fallen into the trap of self-criticizing rather than being critical of societal constructs. You'll recognize that self-criticism in the inner voice narrating everything you do. And such criticism makes this process a challenging one. We may see the obstacles present in ourselves that contribute to us feeling stuck in our lives, and we may see how we lean away from change, holding onto that which is familiar but doesn't serve us – and yet we don't act. The courage and bravery we need to move out of this is found in trusting ourselves. You need to believe that you are able to hold yourself with kindness and non-judgement, whatever happens, as you move forward into the unknown. By experiencing your capacity to be soft and kind and simultaneously strong while dealing with yourself, you begin to find this trust. You will then find you are not falling off the rabbit's fur into the oblivion of the dark unknown when you let go of that which is not serving you. You are held by yourself.

The ideas you may have about who you are are strong but they are not unbreakable. You have already taken the first steps needed to set yourself free from these ideas, as you now know that they are a result of your conditioning. These ideas are no more than a curtain you are hiding behind, while all that time you believed they were a concrete wall. So the next step if you are to let go fully and completely of these ideas is to see very clearly what it is that you'd like to lean into. Visualize this so it feels tangible, as the more you can feel this the safer it will feel to bridge the gap towards change. You need to trade the self-belief system you hold that doesn't serve you for one that does. One that will allow your Inner Spark to glow brightly.

Like I mentioned earlier, these obstacles are universal. We all have to deal with them, as this is simply how our minds are wired. Remember that everyone who's about to step out of emotional struggle, who wants to free themselves, has to overcome the following myths:

1. I'm struggling, so others must think I am crazy.

2. I'm struggling, and no one else is, so I am abnormal.

3. I'm struggling, and I will never again feel like I did before.

4. I'm struggling; I had better get myself together and drag myself out of this all by myself. And if I can't, there's something wrong with me.

Do you recognize any of these statements? Have you ever thought along these lines? That means you're identifying with the struggle. So now let's break these thoughts down.

1. I'm struggling, so others must think I am crazy

No. They certainly don't think so. And you are not crazy. Struggling is human, it's normal. It would be abnormal to not go through difficult periods during a lifetime. To think that you can protect yourself from dark waters and feelings that you don't enjoy would be a sign of avoidance. Life is not something that needs to be controlled so that we only experience certain sentiments, such as happiness. Happiness may not even be what you think it is. It is not something out there to be found or attained. It is how you relate to yourself, your emotions, and your life – especially when things are hard. Desperately grasping whatever you think will make you feel happy actually maintains the feelings of inadequacy and keeps you feeling trapped. So try turning away from that something you think you need to have to be happy. Turn to yourself. To what is going on with you in this moment. And hold yourself with softness and compassion. Be your own best friend. You know that if you saw your very best friend struggling, you'd never think they were crazy, not even for a second. You'd feel for them and wish them goodness, ease, and support.

2. I'm struggling, and no one else is, so I am abnormal

No. Everyone has their struggles. And if it doesn't seem that way, remember this: nothing is as it seems. People go to great lengths to hide their difficulties. This is one of the biggest stigmas we have as a society: that we think we cannot truly show how we are feeling, because then it would be revealed that we are not mastering life. Shame is cruel, but we all fall prey to it. We may even become slaves to it. We overcome shame by reminding ourselves that we are all made of the same stardust and share the same spiritual stories, and we can therefore support each other with compassion. We are group animals, and we thrive in our herds. We support each other best when we are connected in community and in understanding.

3. I'm struggling, and I will never again feel like I did before

Yes, you will. But perhaps not in the way you think. Existentially you are always the same. There is that part of you that never changes, that is the essence of who you are. Yet at the same time, you're always changing. The experiences of life – the imprints left on you by people, situations, and feelings – will all affect you. Remember that one thing we know for sure is that life dances between ease and unease. But even in the midst of the craziest tango ever, you will always remain, in your essence, the same. How we feel at a given moment is a reflection of what is present around us and how we engage with that. It is a reflection also of how we take agency in the relationships we participate in and how we take agency in our surroundings and our situations. How you feel is a result of how you engage with yourself. And although it's easier to be patient and compassionate with yourself in times of ease and when you feel content with your situation, it is also possible to invite this same patience and compassion in at times of unease, understanding yourself, how you feel, where you are mentally in this moment. This is the power of mindfulness and compassion-based practices. They work because we can practise seeing ourselves with gentleness, warmth, and understanding even if we don't feel compassion or understanding immediately. By practising we open the doorway to softness. Practising mindfulness and compassion allows us to feel ease in times of unease. Practising mindfulness pulls us out of the misery, the thick mud of being stuck in emotional struggle, and opens us up to playfulness and Inner Spark.

4. I'm struggling; I had better get myself together and drag myself out of this all by myself. And if I can't, there's something wrong with me.

No. There is nothing wrong with you if you cannot drag yourself out of feeling stuck. There is nothing wrong with you if you can't change the way you think about yourself within the blink of an eye or while looking at yourself in the mirror in the morning. Mind hacks that tell us to 'just think positively' are a hoax and downplay the complexity of our being. Finding our way back to our own agency when we are stuck in emotional struggle takes some serious leaning back and observing. And this can feel counterintuitive since we've been conditioned by contemporary society to be proactive and always do something about what isn't working. We are told to lean forward when what we actually need to do is the opposite. I love the book by Barry Stevens entitled *Don't Push the River (It Flows by Itself)*. The title says it all, but Stevens discusses understanding ourselves especially in times of increasing unease. He argues that the fix you may believe you need in order to release yourself from your struggle is not at all necessary. We don't need more doing and fixing. Doing adds resistance to the situation you are in and resistance to your state of mind and body. And resistance inhibits our leaning into what is actually needed. Resistance to the feelings you have, the situation you are in, and the experiences you have will intensify as you keep grasping at what you desire or at whatever you believe is the solution to your struggle. Resistance increases when you avoid the feelings as they are. And the wall of resistance thickens when you lose hope that you can ride this wave of unease. Resistance builds when you feel unmotivated to inhabit this dance of ease and unease and begin to experience inertia. It's a downward spiral, and quite the paradox. And that is why I want to remind you once again of our innate spirit as group animals. We need each other, we need community, we need a loved one, a friend, a colleague, a spiritual guide, or professional help if we are to move out of emotional struggle. Talk to someone. Share your experience. Sharing some of the energy it carries will begin to bring change. The resistance will begin to crumble as an effect of you opening up and bringing your struggle into words.

In order to free yourself from these universal obstacles and preconceptions, there are a couple of things I'd like to encourage. The Nudge to Action at the end of this chapter will help you to become aware of what your core beliefs are. And to free yourself from the universal obstacles we encounter, consider engaging in the following mindfulness-based RAIN practice on a daily basis.

RAIN Strategy to cope with inner obstacles in your daily life

1. **R**ecognize: take notice of what is there.
2. **A**ccept: allow what you encounter the space it needs.
3. **I**nvestigate: notice how it feels when this is present, physically and emotionally, notice sensations and thoughts, and investigate how it impacts your motivation.
4. **N**on-identification: remember that, as it has appeared, it will also pass.

Core beliefs and erroneous thoughts

A reflection

In this inquiry, you are invited to open up a bit more to yourself and to really start looking into the threads and conditionings that your core beliefs consist of. It's time to remind yourself of the commitment you made to be courageous and of the intention you set for yourself to live from your Inner Spark, so that you can start to step out of your emotional struggle.

Make sure to have your notebook and pencil ready. Find a spot to sit where you feel comfortable: on your meditation cushion (or normal cushion), in your favourite chair, by your favourite window, under a blanket, by a candle, with your favourite tea . . . Take a moment for yourself and create space for this inquiry.

1. Take a moment to settle in. Settle into your body, into your seat. Feel your breath. Notice the space around you. Notice your heart space, right now. Notice how you feel and what emotions are present.

2. What are some beliefs or messages about yourself that come from other people and that you have internalized? Describe these beliefs as briefly as possible.

3. How do these beliefs impact you and where you are in your life right now?

4. What would happen if you were to lean away from where you are right now?

5. What are the core beliefs you have that might hinder you in leaning away from where you are now?

6. When was the last time you felt your Inner Spark?

7. Again, sit for a moment. Close your eyes. Feel your body. Return.

Integration

A practice of connecting the dots

When engaging in the above exercise, was there one thing (or more) you noticed:

- Regarding your breath?
  For example: the rhythm. The depth. Changing of quality. Difference between in breath and out breath. Please describe.

- In your body or connected to bodily sensations?
  For example: one sensation being more intensely present. Or discomfort or comfort. One small area wanting all your attention, or a bigger area of the body. Different sensations, some being more vague, others more clear. Prickling, tickling, or temperature changes. Please describe.

- Regarding the activity of your mind or the movement of thoughts?
  For example: thoughts moving faster or slowly. One idea or situation taking most of your attention, or many thoughts present, maybe jittery. Can you notice the shift of focus of attention? Your quality of mind being clear or more foggy. Please describe.

- In your emotions?
  For example: can you notice any emotion(s) present, arising or passing? Or perhaps the intensity, stronger

or fainter? No analysing where it comes from, or why it is here now. Just noticing what is present. Please describe.

Make sure to read the *Wellbeing Prescription: Pausing* in the final chapter of the book, where function, dosage, and precautions are elaborated.

CHAPTER 6

Readiness for Change
The process of transformation

When the rain pours down, I close my eyes and feel the drops crash onto my face. Small, wet splashes bounce off my skin. I feel the air, crispy and fresh. I see the rain wash the landscape and turn it into a glittering painting, and smell how the wet earth invites me into the presence of this moment. In each and every raindrop the whole of the universe is hidden. So when the rain pours down, I close my eyes and take it all in.

The definition of mental health

In previous chapters, we examined the many layers at which struggles manifest by looking into the qualities of being, the threefold brain, and the tolerance window in which we are able to act wisely and make informed choices. Now we'll reflect for a moment on formal definitions of mental health and move onto how you can take your next steps out of your struggle.

The World Health Organization (WHO) reports regularly on the development of mental health worldwide. Research shows that 25 per cent of the world population will suffer from a mental health disease in their lifetime. Of those who suffer, 75 per cent will never receive help from psychiatric professionals or from the healthcare system. There is a huge gap between what is needed and what is available. Reporting and research by the WHO reveals many more staggering truths. For instance, the numbers of people suffering from widespread issues such as stress, depression, and anxiety are increasing at a worrying rate. The WHO also reports that 50 per cent of these diseases manifest before the age of fourteen. These numbers go a long way in suggesting where intervention is necessary.

The WHO uses a definition of health that dates back to 1946: 'Health is a state of complete physical, mental and social wellbeing and not merely the absence of disease and infirmity.' In the mid-1940s this definition put several human rights issues on the agenda and was beneficial to many groups and societies. However, years later this definition has been criticized. It falls short when seen in the light of the changing paradigms and ways of thinking around mental health in the past decades. For example, the use of the word 'complete' in the definition implies an impossible project. We know for sure that we will be exposed to stressors that we will need to overcome during our lifetimes, and moving through life is impossible without a certain decrease in health. A more correct definition would take into account the natural lifespan shifts and how these affect our health.

The WHO's definition of health is built on the theory of pathologies, which is the description of symptoms as a deviation from a normal state, and a way of describing illnesses. Instead of leaning on pathologies, modern thinking and discourse on mental health leans towards the theory of salutogenesis by medical sociologist Aaron Antonovsky, which shifts the focus from pathology of illnesses to individual empowerment and wellbeing. We could therefore reinterpret the WHO's definition from the perspective of salutogenesis and come up with something like this: 'Good mental health is a state of wellbeing where the individual can realize their potential, and can contribute to others and their immediate society.'

This paradigm shift at the end of the last century in applied psychology and the emergence of humanistic thinking have strengthened the position of positive psychology and its focus on empowerment, and have brought more holistic interventions and approaches to psychotherapy – such as mindfulness-based psychotherapies and compassion-based practices – to the fore. In Buddhist psychology, in particular in the Mahayana lineage, there is a strong focus on theories of neuropsychology, neuroplasticity and polyvagal theory, developmental and attachment theories, and cognitive sciences, and these produce treatment results on a par with other contemporary intervention protocols.

The differences between these interventions and more traditional ones are very important when considering the gap between what is needed and what is available. Mindfulness- and compassion-based practices can bridge this gap for many reasons. For one, these practices are relatively simple to learn. They have a low threshold and are easily accessible. Think of the countless apps, online platforms, and local studios offering instruction, making it relatively easy to maintain a regular practice like this as a complement to treatment. Many apps and community groups are even free or very cheap, which helps to make these practices more available to a wide range of socio-economic groups. In bureaucratic language, these interventions are cost-efficient, easy to learn, and have low-threshold accessibility. They are available to you when you need them, without long wait lists. Also, more and more health insurance companies will reimburse mindfulness-based interventions and yoga therapy.

Readiness for change

We've discussed in previous chapters why change is so much more complex and complicated for us than we might think. We've seen that the most important factor when trying to stand tall in difficult times, during emotional struggle and during setbacks, is the degree to which we can attribute the situation to ourselves. This means, to what extent do we take responsibility for our role in the evolution of our circumstances, and how much of this movement is our own, or is part or all of this caused by our surroundings?

You may have heard this beautiful saying before: 'You don't know the strength of the water until there's a barrier in the river.' Water always finds its way down the mountain. A big rock or any other barrier will not stand in its way and is just an obstacle to overcome. The water has one clear aim, which is to move downwards following the natural law of gravity. That is the water's motivation downstream. There is no hesitation (obviously), the water just moves. Sometimes slowly, drop by drop, and at other times voraciously, with great power. The river is a metaphor for our mental strength.

Just like that river, as humans we are also governed by natural laws. We should consider the law of our own intrinsic motivation as a strong force of nature. Our gravitational pull comes from feeling at ease, feeling safe, and that we belong. This is what we gravitate towards. And just like the water being pulled down the mountain, it is this gravitational pull that helps us feel our real strength when overcoming difficulty. How we embark on that process of overcoming the obstacles in our way is the main predictor of how we will come out of our struggle. For this reason, hope is a vital force of wellbeing and maintaining health. Hope tells us to trust our own abilities and supports us in engaging in the actions needed to move forward. Hope reflects our ability to overcome emotional struggle. Hope strengthens our motivation to move away from wherever we are stuck.

As we've already seen, in order to fully let go of what is not serving us, we need to know something about what awaits us on the other side of the lake. We need to hope (by this I mean trust) that crossing over dark waters will not drown us, but that we can float and swim to the other side. Magically, this process of swimming through the darkness will create a sense of mastery over our own lives, which then lifts us to the other side, to the shore. Of course it is important you are aware of when you need help crossing, and (as I've mentioned before) if you find yourself in deep waters, unable to see or feel any hope of finding your way out of your situation, then do ask for help. Call out for someone to help you stay afloat. And then you can start the process of swimming when the time is right.

The time is right when our motivation or readiness for change is aligned in body, mind, and heart. Then actions, thoughts, and emotions can take the plunge together. We are ready to embark on the actions that are needed, to embark on the process of swimming to the other side, when we feel emotionally safe. And that safety comes when we have understood what that other side might look like. Our mind has untangled and negotiated the pros and cons of giving up our current identities or attachments to our core beliefs. We have started to imagine, perhaps even to visualize, what it will feel like, kinaesthetically, to be on the other side.

Patricia was one of my patients who suffered from depression. We spent many sessions together challenging beliefs arising from a repetitive voice in her head telling her that everything was meaningless and that there was no use in engaging in any activities as they wouldn't change how she felt anyway. She didn't speak up in situations at work because she believed that her opinion was worthless. Colleagues wouldn't pay attention if she spoke, she believed, and that didn't really matter. She didn't matter. So she kept quiet. For years. She internalized, and confirmed for herself this core belief that she was worthless. No one asked her opinion; they let her sit in silence. She only contributed by confirming or mimicking others' opinions, never daring to have her own. The intensity of the self-critical thoughts that attacked her after any utterance resembling an opinion would cause her so much pain and anxiety that it seemed very rarely worth it to her. Her therapeutic work involved mostly negotiating with this inner dialogue so she could become kinder and more compassionate towards herself. She also needed to learn to be patient with herself and challenge her thoughts of meaninglessness and hopelessness. We spent the first ten sessions getting her ready for action. Coming to therapy had been her bravest and greatest act so far. And she kept coming. But the work of letting go of those core beliefs about herself in the world took time.

In the end, how you engage with yourself in difficult times is what is going to make all the difference. How you relate to this difficult feeling of unease, of being stuck, and how you speak to yourself (do you lift yourself up or talk yourself down?), is going to determine how you move forward. If you can lean into hope, if you can commit and recommit to being patient, and if you can find self-compassion in moments of self-criticism, you're on the right track.

Now for the pendulum of ambivalence. Surprisingly, hope can be ambivalent. Any ambivalence we feel towards change is a result of our conditioning and the core beliefs that we hold. The pendulum of ambivalence is driven by how strong our intrinsic motivation to change is. At times when you feel completely and utterly stuck, in a total gridlock, it helps to check in with yourself and evaluate your readiness for change. Often when hopelessness is high, readiness for change is low. When you are aware that your readiness for change is at a certain level, maybe not at the level you need, then you can start inquiring into that. A great tool often used as part of motivational interviews in therapy is the readiness ruler. The readiness ruler is a simple way of checking in with yourself to discover your level of motivation to take action. The ruler is numbered from zero to ten. The aim is to find clarity about which thoughts or convictions hold you captive in your current situation. It's a snapshot of a moment and it can change quickly, even within the space of a day. I'm sure you've experienced this at some point: your confidence in yourself, or your project, can change from one moment to the next. Hopefully that confidence will have increased by the end of the day, but sometimes quite the opposite is the case.

For example, how I've been feeling while writing this book is a great example of the pendulum of ambivalence in action. My confidence about what I'd like to convey and the message I'd like to share has swung all over the place throughout the writing process. This swinging is affected by what I write and how I write it. But mostly this pendulum is affected by how I feel on a particular day. Right now I would say I am somewhere in the middle of the readiness ruler. Some thoughts I am having are: 'There are so many similar books out there – even my teachers have written books like this one. So what do I have to contribute to this topic?' And this is where feelings of inadequacy and shame start to emerge. You can see how this inner dialogue pulls you down towards the zero mark on the readiness ruler. On the other side of the pendulum, a kinder inner voice says: 'I'm writing this for my students and my clients, and I know they'll find this book interesting. This is what they've asked me for, as have colleagues and peers. These people want to hear my voice and my experience.'

The inner argument is not one I will win, yet at the same time I won't lose. Ambivalence can be very confusing but when I can use it to gain knowledge and insight and to investigate the pros and cons of what I am doing, I can become aware of the thoughts that determine my motivational levels in this moment. This helps me understand my inner state better. And it helps me to invite kindness and gentleness in when I feel dark waters threatening to engulf me. Instead of being pulled into the darkness, I see it and I see what it's made of, and I can hold space for myself gently instead of resisting. Instead of rejecting the darker sides of my ambivalence or trying to avoid them, I can see them for what they really are: a set of thoughts.

When you do this, you learn to understand yourself better. This understanding will make you kinder and more compassionate towards yourself in this moment.

. . . .

Did you know . . .
that one of the reasons contemplative and meditative mindfulness and compassion practices work is that they invite us into the moment? They allow us to

experience bottom-up presence, as it is called in cognitive sciences, in which our attention and focus are informed by the kinaesthetic sense, the felt sense, and/or interoception, in the present moment. This is the opposite of our usual state of presence, which is often dictated by a top-down narrative about yourself, your body, and/or your pain. The implicit invitation in such practices is to let go of the ruminating narratives about yourself and who and how you are in this world, at least for a while, and gently be present with yourself in the here and now. As easy as this may sound, it is a challenging practice. We benefit greatly from having a teacher or instructor guide us through it even if we are experienced practitioners, for it is in times of unease that we need this support, we need reminding, and we need guidance.

· ·

Readiness for change

A practice of contemplation and writing

In this exercise you examine your own readiness for change, and what thoughts or feelings are affecting your motivation in this very moment. The exercise sheds light on your current state and is therefore a useful tool that will help you in two ways: you will gain clarity about the underlying mechanisms affecting you in taking action towards change, and you will find more understanding and compassion for yourself in this process.

This exercise has three steps. Please set aside a minimum of 30–60 minutes. You need: a meditation cushion (or normal cushion), a blanket to cover up, a notebook, and a pencil.

Step 1: Connect with yourself

1. Find a comfortable seat somewhere where there are few distractions. Make sure your lower back, hips, and knees are supported.

2. You can close your eyes if you like or rest your gaze softly on the floor.

3. For the next 5–8 minutes, engage in contemplation by observing any phenomena of the mind, arising and passing in your awareness. Whether it is a memory, or a fantasy or worry about the future, or an idea or singular thought jumping around in the mind, simply

observe what is present. Without analysing, figuring out, changing, or removing anything from your attention, just trust that you are doing this correctly. Simply observe the free-associative mind, in this given moment.

4. Your aim in this exercise is to simply notice whatever moves into the spotlight of your attention, and then watch it as it disappears and something new asks for your attention. You don't need to focus on anything in particular. Simply sit and notice what is moving within you. Notice how this affects you as you sit here.

5. To come out of this seated practice, take three deep breaths, inhaling deeply and exhaling fully, before gently opening your eyes and returning to the room.

Step 2: Readiness ruler

1. Find a comfortable way to sit, and take a few moments seated in silence.

2. Have your pen and paper ready. Draw a straight line, and write evenly spaced numbers along it from zero to ten.

3. Consider the issue you are struggling with and what you wish were different. Then ask yourself: how confident am I that I'll reach that different situation where I am no longer struggling? Place yourself on the line you have drawn on the paper next to a number. When you have determined your number, continue asking yourself:

- Why this number right now?

- What are the reasons the number isn't lower?

- What kinds of thoughts are present?

- How does it make me feel?

- What would need to be present for the number to be higher?

- What are the thoughts and feelings behind the intensity of my motivation for change, right now?

4. When you have completed these questions, sit again for a moment in silence.

5. As you wrap up this exercise, know this: when times are tough, your motivation for change can shift dramatically within a day. This is normal. In this phase of bringing awareness to your process, consider using this exercise as a daily practice to check the 'temperature' of your feeling and discover to what extent you are ready to let it go today.

Step 3: Logging out

1. This contemplation practice is can be challenging, so take a moment to sit in silence. Give yourself 5 minutes to log out of this exercise, before returning to your everyday activities.

2. You can close your eyes if you like. What are you noticing right now? How do you feel? After writing all this out, what is present? Just notice what is

present right now. In your thoughts, your feelings, in your body. Sit with yourself in silence for a moment.

3. And to come back, take a few deeper breaths, and return to the room, opening your eyes, when you feel ready.

Integration

A practice of connecting the dots

When engaging in the above exercise, was there one thing (or more) you noticed?

- Regarding your breath?
  For example: the rhythm. The depth. Changing of quality. The difference between inhale and exhale. Please describe.

- In your body or connected to bodily sensations?
  For example: a sensation being more intensely present. Some discomfort or comfort. One small area wanting all your attention, or a bigger area of the body. Different sensations, some subtle, others obvious. Prickling, tickling, or temperature changes. Please describe.

- Regarding the activity of your mind or the movement of thoughts?
  For example: thoughts moving fast or slowly. One idea or situation demanding your attention. Or were there many thoughts present, maybe scattered or jittery. Did you notice a shift of focus or attention? Did your quality of mind become clearer or more foggy? Please describe.

- In your emotions?
  For example: did you notice any emotion(s) Did you

notice any emotions arising and passing? Fading?
Or perhaps you became aware of the intensity of
emotions becoming stronger or lighter? Please
describe.

Remember, try not to analyse where it came from, or why it is here now. Just notice what is present.

Agency

Now you have opened the door to gentleness and kindness and more understanding towards yourself, the time has come for you to move forward in your process of stepping out of your struggle. This gentleness is a sign that you are indeed ready to move forward: in finding it you have discovered that stepping out of your current state is more beneficial to you than staying in it. In addition, you've discovered what you need in order to make this shift. At this point, you have reached your agency and enabled yourself to gently move into action.

The French philosopher and psychoanalyst Anne Dufourmantelle wrote a beautiful description of gentleness: 'Gentleness is a force of secret life-giving transformation linked to what the ancients called "potentiality". Without it there is no possibility for life to advance in its becoming.'

This elegant phrasing of gentleness illustrates that change cannot be forced. When we encounter transitions in life, we are faced simultaneously with challenging psychological processes and with difficult emotions. This asks us to approach difficulty with gentleness and compassion and to engage in an attitude that isn't the prevalent choice in Western society. We are used to 'grabbing the bull by the horns', being proactive and ambitious, and reacting to desire and/or aversion. But we know that acting when we aren't yet ready – especially in change processes – is counterproductive. When you go to your doctor or to a therapist or even to a friend, looking for help, you're probably thinking: 'Fix me. Take away this problem.' Yet what is needed most is for you to be patient with yourself and with the experience of feeling stuck. This moment can be seen as an act of kindness to silence the inner critic and open the door to self-compassion, and an invitation to meet yourself and your inner landscapes (both light and dark) as your own best friend. No one can fix you – except you. That radical freedom you are looking for is right there within you. It is in your own heart, you just have to see it. Give it attention and nurture it so your Inner Spark can shine through.

The trick is to let go of the conviction that something outside of yourself is needed for you to make that shift. You don't need something or someone to change so that you can step out of your struggle. The shift will happen when you are ready for change. And that is when blocked feelings can be brought to the surface and can be expressed. Your feelings have become meaningful to you: their purpose and function are revealed. The integration of new insights can begin, and this heightened awareness then informs your actions. You can make skilful choices for yourself and act upon them because of your newfound awareness. It's like you have been pushed through a myopic tunnel and come out the other side with your vision clear and wide. Readiness for change can be seen as an effect of moving through this tunnel; when you reach the other side you become more integrated with your whole self. Your experience of being stuck makes sense, and your experience that previously felt fragmented and singular becomes part of the whole of you. Your experience of struggle actually ends up making you whole again. And then when you consider the efforts you want to make and the outcome of these to be safe (read: predictable), you can let go of what is currently causing you to struggle emotionally.

....

Did you know...
that relationships are one of the most significant predictors of longevity? As shown in a 2016 longitudinal study by Yang Claire Yang et al., they impact our sense of wellbeing not only psychologically but also physiologically. As a result we may conclude that not only the quality of your social relationships but also how you relate to yourself are of significance to your overall sense of wellbeing and contentment in life. This means that the more you know about yourself, and the more knowledge you have of the underlying forces of motivation and mechanisms of agency, the greater your life expectancy.

....

Let me give you an example. A mother of three children under six was feeling disconnected from her husband. She was stressed out in this hectic phase of life, juggling work, motherhood, and the logistics of family life. She was doing exactly what recent studies show often happens: she had effectively taken on a third job (in addition to her work and her role as a mother) in organizing family life. Women often do much more of this than men, and she was no exception. She came to my practice to treat the panic attacks she had started to experience. She was convinced it was the inadequacy of her husband that was causing her this stress. She felt he didn't help her with anything, whereas she was drowning in stress. She said he didn't see any of the things she did or the pressure she was experiencing, and she also felt like he didn't see her at all. She started to feel repulsed by him and felt herself slipping into a downward spiral. When she came to therapy she believed the solution to her struggles was to get a divorce. She was convinced he was the root of her problems and that she would be able to handle the hectic daily stress better if he were no longer in the equation. Without him, there would be one less factor for her to take into account. He never did what she thought was right and he rarely did what she asked him. He would actually do the opposite, and in doing so reject her. She was more educated than her husband and was working full-time in a more demanding job and also making more money than he was. Yet she was also the one coordinating the family logistics in her head. After many sessions, she admitted that being in control was her default survival mode. She simply had too much on her plate, yet she wouldn't consider handing some of these tasks over to her husband. She had to step back for him to step in, but the only solution she could come up with for her problem was that her husband was incompetent and he had to go. So she let him go. A year later she was still unhappy, stressed, and now also lonelier than before. Even though her husband may have not been the most competent partner, she had failed to address her true issue: the belief that controlling her environment and surroundings would affect her levels of happiness. The mere idea set her up for failure and was the primary reason she experienced emotional struggles and felt stuck. A year after she left her husband, she returned to therapy. Her challenge this time was to look into her loneliness and change the thought patterns that kept her feeling stuck, and of course her fear of losing control.

The process of transformation

The process of leaning into darker waters, away from emotional struggles, and towards Inner Spark has several steps. The steps are inspired by psychoanalysts Prochaska and DiClemente's transtheoretical model 'The process of change', and bring awareness to the fact that transformational processes have several phases. How long is spent in each phase will vary, but the important thing is to what degree you are engaged in your process, not how long each phase lasts. The movement between the phases should flow organically but not necessarily chronologically; moving back and forth is not unusual. Below is a list of the phases to help you recognize them and hopefully add to your understanding and patience with yourself.

The organic phases in a process of change

1. Realization of struggle

In this phase you realize that the quality of your current state is causing your struggle. It becomes clear you are in a situation that is not serving you, that what is present is painful and detrimental to your health and your ability to function and express yourself fully in life. In this phase you address that there is struggle in your daily life, and hopefully you can also describe it to the best of your ability.

2. Wish to change

In this phase you feel that inner nudge of wanting your situation to be different. You can articulate that you do not wish to stay in the state of unease, and that you would like to live in a state of more ease. Perhaps you can even verbalize what you wish to be different, what you wish to see changed or don't want any more. In this phase you are connected to your own engagement on a path towards ease.

3. Insights of meaningfulness

As you engage in self-care and invite moments of ease in, you are preparing to fully embody the struggle you are experiencing, your inner dark. With sufficient reflection, contemplation, meditation, or therapeutic work, insights into the complexity of your situation come to you with clarity. You reach a new awareness of your situation, connecting the dots in your current narrative about yourself so that they have meaning. You see your struggle in a larger context, your pain becomes purposeful, and you are ready to move towards the next phase in the process of change. Feeling stuck transforms into a more gentle quality as we start perceiving the meaning of this feeling in our lives. The constructs of the mind or conditionings that support the struggle are revealed and, knowing these, you can start the work.

4. Consideration: the pendulum of ambivalence

The work involves you considering the pros and cons of what you'll gain and lose by stepping out of your current state. The negotiations begin. You negotiate with your own motivation on what you'll gain by leaning away from what you know and what is not serving you, towards what you don't know but have assessed will probably be a healthier choice for you. In this phase, you'll spend time collecting information (perhaps through visualization) on what your future could look like or feel like. The clearer and more tangible your goals are the less effort you'll need to reach them and the easier it will be for you to assess what you need to get there. This phase is about seeing and embracing all parts of yourself, including the parts you do not like, the darker waters, and the parts that contribute to holding you in your struggle.

5. Agency to action

This is when you have acquired sufficient information about where you're heading, and you trust that you have what it takes to move there. You trust yourself and your resources, and you embody yourself with patience and gentleness. This means you have widened your window of tolerance for your own difficult emotions, and you allow them the space they need. You allow yourself to feel what is there fully. You are also able to understand and verbalize them, or to express them in some other constructive or skilful way, so that you can move forward gently and gracefully. You take the steps needed to move towards where you want to be.

6. Integration

This is when the shift has happened and you have landed on two feet on the other side. This phase requires continuous engagement. Integration is not a place you land and stay; you could easily be flung back. Integration is the effect of continuous inquiry, engagement, and action, with the intention of nourishing your emotional health and maintaining your Inner Spark. This is essential because, in the process of stepping out of the struggle, you are the primary agent of your emotional wellbeing. How you engage with what you experience, and how continuously you engage, will impact your overall health.

Surfing the waves of emotion

First we pause, then insights will come to us like sweet drops of honey. In mindfulness-based practices we learn that our focus of attention can move from one object to another and that we can shift the focus of our attention deliberately. This is how we learn the practice of selective attention. When we have practised this for a while, simultaneously practising an attitude of kindness and non-judgement, we take the next step.

We learn how to sit with whatever is passing in our inner landscapes in a given moment. This is the meta-perspective, seeing the objects in our mind within a larger context. We become a neutral observer, or a witness to whatever is going on in our minds as if we were watching a movie; thoughts, memories, and fantasies are like the images on the screen. The technique of bringing your attention to a certain object – like breath or bodily sensations or an object in front of you – is a tool that grounds you in the present moment. We can use this tool to always come back to the body and this can be necessary when the movie we are watching becomes too intense. When the movie in the mind creates or aggravates intense emotions, we can get dragged onto centre stage and lose that meta-perspective. Coming back into the body helps us in these situations.

Difficult emotions can be like a whirlpool, spiralling you into unease. This can be a dizzying experience and can be hard to escape. Simply accepting the arising and passing of this intensity can be very challenging, especially if we didn't see this wave of emotion coming.

To overcome such waves we need emotional resilience. We know that this resilience can be built by practising various exercises over time. These exercises strengthen our emotional stamina and tolerance so that we can surf that wave when it comes. We practise when the water is still. Then, when the waters start to become turbulent and the waves start growing, we have the techniques we need and we won't be dragged under.

Building emotional resilience requires mental space. To find and grow mental space, we need sufficient time and we also need what I like to call potent pauses. You know those moments: when mental space opens up as though you can feel your turbulent inner landscapes leaning back. These are moments in which you can rest in the meta-perspective. So you are not *in* the whirlpool but witnessing it. Instead of being overwhelmed by the crashing waves, you are steadily riding them, gently and continuously – you have found ease in the unease.

There are some beautiful and simple practices to open up this space. Let's try one.

Potent pauses

A writing practice

In this practice, you'll invite yourself into tranquillity and gentleness, and take stock of potent pauses you feel are accessible to you. Potent pauses are activities that nourish you and make you feel more at ease.

1. **Connect**: Find a comfortable seat. Take a moment to settle in the here and now. Close your eyes or rest your gaze softly on the floor. Pause here, just sit and breathe.

2. **Ease**: Take your pen and paper and write sentences starting with 'Last time I felt free and flowing was when . . .' Describe the situation that comes to mind as thoroughly as you want. Write about at least three situations. I encourage you to describe the following for each of these situations:

   - How did the situation make you feel/what emotions were present?

   - Where were you in that moment?

   - How did your body feel?

   - What kinds of thought were present?

3. **Self-care**: Next, make a list of five to ten activities that you know give you a solid pause from mind-driven

behaviours. This is a list of activities that you would consider self-care. Things you enjoy doing that give you joy and make you feel good but that you have not prioritized for whatever reason (such as time limitations). Feel free to make this a decorative list, and hang it on your wall as a daily reminder or put it in your wallet. Or both!

Make sure to read the *Wellbeing Prescription: Perspective* in the final chapter of the book, where function, dosage, and precautions are elaborated.

PART III

Agency

Moving with intention:
Skilful effort and making
the right choices

CHAPTER 7

How to Step Out of Struggle
Eight steps of agency

Have you seen how the mountain changes as the rays of light reflect on the rocks? How shadows and creeks of darkness suddenly reveal their secrets? How the grey stones suddenly shine like a jewel? How the spiky tops reveal themselves to be smooth and gentle formations? And how the highest peaks, raging dangerously in the skies, become viewing points for the most magical landscapes your eyes have ever rested upon?

In Parts I and II of the book we put down a solid framework to help you understand yourself and your current situation. We pulled away the layers of what you have little to no control over, revealing what you do have some control over, and began to sense our real power: our agency. Now in this last part of the book we'll be diving into how to take charge and really create a shift in your situation. I hope you've had time to do the practices and Nudges to Action in this home-based retreat. Know that you can always revisit these practices whenever you want.

Live in your landscape

Bodø. This is the name of the city, just north of the Arctic Circle, where I was born and raised. The word Bodø is made up of two words: *bo* and *dø*, which literally mean 'living' and 'dying'. The origin of the city's name refers to the farm that the city was built on and around, and is a reference to the landscape. It means 'living on an island', as Bodø is situated on a peninsula. The living and dying found within the name, however, makes for a more poetic framework, and I personally feel this embodies this ravaging, magical, and majestic landscape far better. There's a savage beauty in its roughness.

As I'm sure you have noticed, I have a special relationship with this place, and I feel deeply connected to nature here. I am sure we all have a special connection in one way or another to the land we come from. For me, having travelled the world and lived in many different countries and sceneries, the poetry of landscapes fascinates me. And what it does to us and to our inner landscapes is just as fascinating to me. I love returning home to the north. It always feels like returning to paradise.

Just like the Eastern schools of thinking and the philosophies behind mindfulness- and compassion-based practices, nature gifts us some solid teachings. The first time I brought my husband up north, I had to let him in on a few secrets about living in the Arctic. He was (and still is) into sandy white beaches, reaching as far as the eye can see, fringed by crystal blue waters. And we have that here. Alluring, right? However, up here the water is always effing cold, to say the least. Even in summers, when beaches are full with temperatures above 30°C (yes, it happens) and you want to take a refreshing dip, that water is going to make you feel like you are in the throes of a cardiac arrest. In Scandinavia ice-water bathing is actually a popular wellness activity, especially in winter.

One of those secrets of living up north was that there's no bad weather, only bad clothing. As mundane as this may sound, it has a profound message that I believe says something about the attitude of the people here. It reveals an attitude that is essential for us if we are to cope and live through the darkness of the winter and the endless presence of the summer light. Keeping in tune with nature is key. Living in this environment, in these landscapes, we adapt. We could keep checking our app to find out when the rain is going to stop, but it is very unlikely that the app will adequately predict the weather here. Dependence on an app means you'll risk waiting in despair. Here, we live in the storm, we take hikes in the rain, we go jogging on the ice (well, not me, as I'm not much of a runner). We pull on our spiky sneakers and we (they) run. We climb the mountains, carefully. And we jump into the ice-cold water. We talk about the weather as though it were a person: 'He was strong last night is what we say about a storm that fell just short of ripping our roofs off. And we spend time in nature. As it is. Without waiting for the right weather.

Adapting to our circumstances and our environment is one of our specialities as a species. However, it's important to remember this adapting is not happening at the expense of our wellbeing.

....

Did you know ...

that swimming in cold water could be good for your mental health? Once you get over the feeling of freezing your ass off, it can be quite invigorating to swim in cold water. Hydrotherapy actually dates back to ancient times, when it was thought that exposing the skin to water of various temperatures could alleviate heavy moods. Today, some claim cold-water swimming reduces symptoms of depression and anxiety. Preliminary research shows positive effects, though this theory has yet to be studied in a more structured manner with larger study groups and over longer periods of time. In the meantime, you can always do your own research and become the subject of investigation. Expose yourself to cold waters and note how this makes you feel! Both biophilic and attention-restoration theories support that this exposure should have benefits. Biophilic theory shows increased productivity and health benefits through contact with nature, supporting the hypothesis that we thrive when connected to nature and other living beings.

. . . .

Commitment to self-agency

For those of you who have practised yoga or mindfulness-based practices for a while, you know that it requires some commitment to practise meditative and contemplative exercises regularly. You must commit to continuous self-inquiry as a way of life. You commit to unravelling the conditionings of the mind, as we are faced with them again and again in new shapes and forms, as thoughts and actions. We are able to commit to this self-inquiry because we know it teaches us a little more about ourselves each day and it helps us find ease in times of unease. Leaning into our gentleness and patience allows us to access our agency and enables us to find the tools we need to step out of emotional struggle. As we lean towards more self-compassion, understanding ourselves and our situation, we see that holding onto ideas and beliefs about being stuck is what holds us captive in our state of unease.

In this chapter we will look into the eight aspects of agency that will help you meet yourself with kindness and will help you when you feel stuck. These are reminders as well as action points. If you wish to see change for yourself, to be free from the emotional struggle and the unease you are experiencing, you will need to work on each of these steps. You will need to move with awareness and evaluate how these steps work for you right now. It is up to you to see if you are employing these tools in a manner that serves you or if you are somehow contributing to your feeling of being stuck. No one else can do this for you. If you find this difficult, you can ask for help or support in this process. But the actual *doing* is your work and no one else's. This will probably be the most challenging part of this process for you, and I hope you can take a moment now to kindly remind yourself to stay close to your sense of gentleness.

Eight aspects of agency

There is a lot of good advice available to help you move out of emotional struggle. The best and most efficient advice involves taking responsibility for yourself. This is known as agency. Emotional health and the maintenance of this health, and increasing your emotional wellbeing, requires your own efforts. The following eight aspects of agency are inspired by a translation of Buddha's eightfold path, which was given to me by my teachers at Spirit Rock. These points should help you sort out your inner chaos and reduce the sense of feeling overwhelmed, as you learn to sort and order, placing your experiences and feelings where they belong, in the right place and in perspective. When this is done you can lean fully into your dark waters, feeling held and secure, and tidy up that inner chaos. You will free yourself from emotional struggle and unease by employing skilful tools.

The eight aspects are not exercises meant for you to excel in. They are characteristics of your presence, your relationship with yourself, and your daily life for you to contemplate. Use them to inquire into whether there are ways for you to be more attuned to this moment. The skills you employ need to be in tune with your needs, the phase of life you are in, your overall health situation, your financial situation, and your relationship situation. There's nothing to be achieved here, no goal to set, except to remind yourself of where you are so you can keep your attention clear. Especially in times of transition, when emotions can be intense, it is important that inner fluctuations are expressed and regulated. Transitions are not once-in-a-lifetime events. This is what it means to be alive; movement and transition are continuous, whether referring to the people we meet and love, to ourselves and our inner and outer experiences, or our hearts. That is life.

The following eight aspects of agency are useful to remind yourself of in times of difficulty, especially when you feel an increased desire to control your situation and when uneasy feelings start creeping up on you. Use these aspects – not necessarily in this order – to reflect on and to widen your perspective. Do this gently.

The eight aspects are interrelated and work on multiple

levels simultaneously. They are expressed at the individual level (or intrapersonal: me, myself, and I). They are also expressed interpersonally, meaning in your closest relationships. Finally, they are expressed at the societal level. All three levels are in play at once, and they impact each other. How you relate and feel towards yourself impacts how you see and interact with people around you, how you perceive your surroundings, and how you move in them. Similarly, the state of your surroundings and the quality of your relationships will impact how you feel. You can evolve regardless of where you are, with whatever resources and genetics you have been given. You can explore and work on these aspects of self-agency, bringing yourself towards greater emotional wellbeing and mental sustainability.

The eight aspects to examine in order to enable more agency and skilful ways of relating to yourself and the people and environment around you are: skilful speech; skilful action; skilful livelihood; skilful effort; skilful mindfulness; skilful concentration; skilful understanding; skilful thinking. The first three aspects I will describe are related to the underlying ethics of our behaviour and how this behaviour is guided. They refer to how we choose to be in this world, or how we engage in it.

1. Skilful speech

Skilful speech is when we are able to overcome the inner voice of self-judgement and talking ourselves down. Our minds are wired to cling to negative feedback and comments rather than positive ones. Remember that the scarcity principle ensures the brain focuses on what is missing, encouraging behaviours that will 'right' the 'wrong'. For example, depressed body language sends a message of sadness and loneliness, and communicates to anyone around us that comfort and closeness is needed. This same mechanism ensures we hear negative feedback instead of positive feedback, and the negative is supposed to motivate us towards action and change. There's a tendency, however, to cling to and drown in the critical comments we bombard ourselves with in a lifetime. We weave these comments into our inner voice and they become critical speech and beliefs against ourselves. Speaking to ourselves in this way does not serve us in the long run.

Skilful speech is held by ease. It will allow you to respond from compassion, curiosity, and kindness rather than from criticism and reaction. Skilful speech is an art and requires practice, both when applied interpersonally (between you and others) and intrapersonally (within yourself, which is perhaps even more challenging).

As we saw in earlier chapters, regarding yourself with compassion and kindness becomes increasingly difficult as unease becomes more intense. And the inner voice tends to tag along, becoming more critical as you experience more difficult emotions. This can result in a downward spiral. We'll look at this in more depth in Chapter 8, but for now why don't you begin to notice how you speak to yourself (internally) for the rest of the day? Are you talking yourself up? Or down? What words do you use to talk to yourself? Are you judgemental in your choice of words? Or do you speak with respect?

2. Skilful action

Skilful action – or choosing more skilful ways to act – is often easier said than done. It is again a matter of leaning into gentleness, choosing ease rather than fighting yourself and resisting. As we've seen before, breaking free from those conditionings and habitual patterns is a tedious process and requires a lot of energy. Let's look at what these skilful actions can be.

First of all, skilful actions are those that clearly serve you right now. There is an emphasis on the word 'now'. They may not be what you needed last year or what will be skilful ten years from now.

Skilful actions are health-promoting and give you goodness. To be able to engage in skilful actions, a knowledge of what you need is important.

Here are some examples of actions you might need:

- engaging in self-care activities or more formalized self-care actions

- setting boundaries

- questioning challenging relationships

- making firm decisions

- acquiring new knowledge

- not doing anything at all

When we experience high degrees of inner unease, we can feel stuck in repetitive thoughts. As you look for a way out, you can see the door, but every time you get close to it your legs carry you away for yet another round of rumination. You are caught in the autopilot of your mind and you keep running around in circles. Sometimes to access that door and move through it you need someone else to open it for you. Or perhaps someone else to nudge you out of the seemingly never-ending loop of rumination. The strongest kind of bravery I see in people is when they say: 'I need help. I'm stuck. I'm hurting. I think I know some of the reasons, but I need help. I just cannot get out of this on my own. Please show me how.' Asking for help is truly skilful action at its best. To admit to yourself that trying to find your way all by yourself is not serving you is a huge step. Asking for help is the most skilful thing you can do.

Think about your current situation and how you are trying to solve it: would it benefit you to ask for help?

3. Skilful livelihood

To have work or a job that you enjoy and feel fulfilled by is quite something. Skilful livelihood does not mean, however, that you should find out what you are most passionate about and make your living from that as a means of fulfilling your potential. Instead, see skilful livelihood as a job, or a way of making a living, in which effort and outcome serve you and your loved ones in a balanced manner. What you do should support yourself, others, and society in a wholesome way. An example of non-skilful livelihood, for instance, would be making or selling weapons. Or anything that damages nature or is non-sustainable for your community. Anything that is non-wholesome or non-serving.

Throughout our lives we change a lot, and consequently our needs change as well. The essence of us will remain constant, but what we value as important can fluctuate. Therefore, what you might at one point have enjoyed very much as your livelihood could change dramatically with time. As mentioned, our societies encourage self-realization through work, telling us we can do whatever we want. I disagree with that. Reaching for the unknown can be more unnerving and confusing than anything else.

The idea that life begins outside your comfort zone – that we should be constantly pushing our limits – is not very helpful. This idea strengthens the belief that wherever you are now isn't good enough. So I'd encourage you to check in with yourself and see where you are right now: what do you have available, and what do you need? Use this to guide you instead of reaching towards the unknown, the somewhere out there. Sometimes we need to make our world a little smaller and more available to us rather than looking at the unattained. We can build on the resources we have right now. Skilful livelihood should not be seen in a vacuum. It does not refer to the best job, career, or project for you. It refers to livelihood on so many levels.

Here are a few questions to keep in mind:

- Is this serving me? How?

- Is this serving my family or immediate community? How?

- Is this serving society as a whole? How?

The next three aspects are related to the quality of your presence when interacting with your loved ones (including yourself) and with your surroundings. It is about your mental presence, your focus of attention, attitude, and quality of mind.

4. Skilful effort

I love this one: skilful effort, which comes down to regulating your energy. I often check in with myself on this, especially during hectic times. And I think it is vital if you want to take agency when you feel overwhelmed by all the things on your to-do list. It is incredibly important to investigate how you do the things you do and the amount of energy you put into your effort. It is not what we do, but how we do it, that will determine the effect it has on us.

One of my teachers gave me this beautiful advice: when you do something, check in with yourself. How much energy (mentally and physically) does this really require from you? And how much energy are you actually spending on it? For example, look at the things you do every day, like laundry or tidying up your home, getting groceries and cooking (and thinking about what to make); or look at your work, how you go through your emails or other activities, and think about what kind of effort you put into it. Do you go at it with 10-horsepower effort when it actually just needs 1 horsepower?

In examining the perfectionistic paradigm earlier, we exposed a romantic image of being busy. Multitasking has been put on a pedestal, and our accomplishments are seen as measures of success and happiness. I have never heard a patient say, 'I do too little.' I have, however, heard plenty saying that they cannot find ease in themselves and relax. Even when sitting, or just lying down on the couch and supposedly resting, they don't feel relaxed. Chaotic thoughts persevere. Their shoulder and neck muscles are tight. They feel as if there's a heavy stone in the belly, they feel pressure on the chest. While fanatically watching Netflix, they still feel stressed.

A patient said to me the other day: 'This impatience rules me. It tells me to do things quickly and simultaneously. It makes me happy. Or no, content. Or no. No. It makes me stressed out. But my inner voice keeps telling me to get things done anyway. Get this or that out of the way. And because of that voice I am very efficient! And then after it's all done, I can relax.' I responded: 'But you just said that you cannot find relaxation when you eventually sit down. Whose voice is it really, that inner voice telling you to get things done?' She paused for a moment. 'Yeah. It's my father's voice.' And then she sighed deeply and let the tears flow.

Throughout the rest of your day, I invite you to take notice of what kind of effort you put into the things you do. How do you feel while moving through your activities, and do you feel aligned with your energy levels and the effort needed to get things done?

5. Skilful mindfulness

Skilful mindfulness is also known as the attitude of attention. This aspect of self-agency is beautiful and oh so tricky. It entails not only what you think and how you feel about yourself, but most importantly how you relate to yourself. In what way do you embody yourself? With what quality? What approach? Mindfulness is defined within this aspect as an attitude of kindness and acceptance rather than judgement, and as a presence in the here and now. Skilful mindfulness is thus an attitude of attention in the present, and refers to how you relate to yourself and the content of your inner landscapes.

This is especially important when it comes to the parts of yourself that you are not loving or perhaps not liking. Think about this for a moment: how do you relate to those parts? How do you embody them? Are you trying to avoid them? Are you ignoring them? Intentionally or unconsciously? What is your chosen attitude: control and resistance, or patience and gentleness?

The same goes for the people around you. Perhaps your loved ones do something you don't approve of. Or maybe you have colleagues you don't really like. Skilful mindfulness or the quality of your attitude makes a difference. I'm sure you've noticed this in the various relationships and interactions in your life. For example, in your professional life, how do you pay attention and how do you express your attention in the presence of your supervisor? And what about a co-worker? Or what is your attitude when you are with your grandparents or your parents, compared to your partner or your children? We present ourselves differently based upon what we believe others need or expect from us. And skilful mindfulness tells us to become aware of our attitudes as we meet others and ourselves and bring clear-minded intention into these meetings.

Take a moment to check in with yourself. What attitude did you have towards yourself today? And towards your partner? Or your colleagues? Are you moving on autopilot, or are you bringing yourself to each interaction mindfully?

6. *Skilful concentration*

Now we've covered how we focus our attention and the attitude behind our attention, we can move on to skilful concentration, or the focus of attention. This refers to what we focus our attention on – our selective attention. This ability is regulated by our prefrontal cortex and means we can shift our focus of attention deliberately.

For example, if we are caught in a downward spiral of thoughts, worries, or fears, we can move our focus of attention onto something else. An often-used mindfulness practice that illustrates this is the passing cloud exercise: imagine that your thoughts are clouds and that you can watch them as they appear, gliding into your attention, and then disappear from your sight again. This practice requires you to step into the perspective of an observer. You make space and step away from the actual thought. It invites you into a meta-perspective in which you can be aware of your thinking instead of being overwhelmed by your thoughts.

Let's give it a try, first with external objects. What can you see right now? What kinds of shapes? Are the objects large or small? Near or far? Then listen: what sounds can you hear right now? Are they high-pitched, low-pitched, far away, nearby? Just as we can move our attention from one sensory organ to another, we can shift our focus of attention between sensory information or bodily sensations, to thoughts or emotions, taking on the perspective of the observer.

7. *Skilful thought*

Skilful thought is another aspect to bring more awareness to. This is not about right or wrong thinking. It is about becoming aware of the intentions behind your thinking. So perhaps it would be more accurate to call it right intention.

Skilful thought surfaces in how you attribute a situation: how you perceive your own role, your ability to control the situation, and what you believe you should be doing in the situation. Skilful thinking is related to how you see your own agency or responsibility, and how you relate to the situation. Is this happening to you? Are you a random bystander? How do you meet yourself in the situation? Are you able to engage skilfully, in alignment with your intentions?

For example, skilful thought would not allow you to surrender to a whirlpool of negative erroneous thoughts about yourself or your position in this world. It is realizing that you can step out of the whirlpool and reset the intention you are acting from. You then recalibrate your actions accordingly. Skilful thought means becoming aware of your state of mind and becoming the observer of the mind.

8. Skilful understanding

Skilful understanding means you take into consideration what your concerns are in this moment, where they come from, and how they impact you or obstruct you in moving forward, and finally how you overcome your current concerns. This covers just about everything we've discussed so far in the book.

Skilful understanding encompasses the view you have of yourself, of the world, and of yourself in the world. You observe what your perspective is and how you behave and act from that. This includes the awareness of knowing your feelings in a given situation. And it also includes awareness of how you respond: are you able to observe with an equanimous mind or do you become reactive? And skilful understanding also means you are able to acknowledge and respect others' perspectives, especially when they differ from yours.

Think about a recent conflict situation you were in, perhaps a fight you had with someone. What was your understanding of this conflict while you were in the midst of it? What is your understanding of it now? Can you understand the perspective of the other person?

Skilful understanding is your ability to consider that people are separate individuals with different inner landscapes, ways of thinking, feelings, and needs. It touches on your ability to be an empathic being.

Movement poetry

A movement practice of mindful yoga (15–30 minutes)

This Nudge to Action is one of my personal favourites. It allows a gentle connection with yourself and stimulates your senses, especially the sixth sense – the kinaesthetic sense, or felt sense of the body.

1. **The body**: Lie down on your back on the floor. Now make a star shape with your body by stretching your arms out to the sides and your legs away from each other. With each inhale, lengthen and stretch as much as you can and push the back of your body down into the floor. On the exhale, release and relax. Repeat five times (or more if you like).

2. **The face**: Make facial movements tensing and stretching the face, shutting the eyes tightly and clenching the jaw (grimacing), then open your eyes wide and open the mouth and jaw widely. Repeat five times (or more if you like).

3. **The eyes**: Roll the eyes up, down, side to side, diagonally up to the right, down to the left, then up to the left and down to the right. Then roll your eyes in full circles, then roll them the other way. Repeat two times (or more if you like).

4. **The neck**: Sit upright with your head balancing on

top of the spine. Inhale deeply, and exhale and turn your head to the right. Inhale and bring it back to the centre, then exhale and turn to the left. Keep going like this for a few rounds of breath. Then begin to tilt the head from side to side, bringing your ear to your shoulder, also in synchronicity with your breath. To finish, you can make circles with your head, first one way then the other. Repeat two times (or more if you like).

5. **The spine**: Come onto all fours (hands and knees). Check that your knees are hip width apart and your hands are at shoulder width. Inhale and lift your chest and gaze upwards so that your lower back hollows. Exhale and bring your gaze to your belly, rounding your spine by drawing your tailbone in. Repeat five times (or more if you like).

6. **Standing tall**: Stand with your feet hip width apart. Inhale and lengthen your arms up towards the ceiling, pushing your feet into the floor. Exhale and let the arms fall down alongside your body. Repeat five times (or more if you like).

7. **Dance!** Put on some music that you enjoy, and dance around with the mere intention of enjoyment and moving your body.

8. **Take rest**: When you feel ready, lie down, cover yourself with a blanket if you like, and take a moment to rest.

For more yoga practices, you can visit www.thehouseofyoga. com.

Integration

A practice of connecting the dots

When engaging in the above exercise, was there one thing (or more) you noticed?

- Regarding your breath?
  For example: the rhythm. The depth. Change of quality. The difference between inhale and exhale. Please describe.

- In your body or connected to bodily sensations?
  For example: a sensation being intensely present. Some discomfort or comfort. One small area asking for all your attention, or a larger area of the body. Different sensations, some subtle, others obvious. Prickling, tickling, or temperature changes. Please describe.

- Regarding the activity of your mind or the movement of thoughts?
  For example: thoughts moving fast or slowly. One idea, thought or situation demanding your attention. Or were there many thoughts present, maybe scattered or jittery. Did you notice a shift in focus or attention? Did your quality of mind become clearer or more foggy? Please describe.

- In your emotions?
  For example: did you notice any emotion(s)? Did you notice any emotions rising and passing? Fading? Or

perhaps you became aware of the intensity of emotions becoming stronger or lighter. Please describe.

Remember, try not to analyse your answers or to explain where sensations come from or why they are arising. Just notice what is present.

Make sure to read the *Wellbeing Prescription: Movement poetry* in the final chapter of the book, where function, dosage, and precautions are elaborated.

CHAPTER 8

Who Are You Now?
Telling your story with your own words

When the sun's rays break through the clouds and beam down on the ancient landscapes, their magnificent brilliance hits like a magical wave. The rays light up the landscapes, revealing the stories of everyone who ever lived here.

The ontology of being a human

We don't exist in a vacuum. We see ourselves as part of the surroundings we live and function in. We identify in relation to the people we interact with, those who mean something to us and to whom we mean something too. It is essential for our wellbeing that we are valued by others and have meaning in the lives of others. Remember that research has shown that a feeling of belonging is one of the most important factors affecting lifespan, and that meaningful relationships are an important predictor of longevity. In order to feel happy, what we mean to the people in our lives – meaning how they see us – and how we understand ourselves need to be aligned. This is a beautiful example of how simple we actually are as beings, even though we see ourselves as quite complex. We simply need our tribe, our community – our *sangha*.

Who you are

The essence of Inner Spark is how you relate to yourself, especially in times of emotional struggle. Inner Spark is a path towards discovery of your attitude towards yourself, finding perspective in your inner dialogue, and ultimately changing your attitude and that dialogue. I believe it's not *who* you are, but *what* you do and *how* you do it, that will determine who you are in a given moment. How you meet the emotional struggle within yourself, how you find ease in unease, will determine who you are. And this is connected to your Buddha nature and the realization that you are already integrated as a whole and full being. That Inner Spark is an innate part of you; you are innately of this nature.

From the moment we are born, our stories begin to be narrated. Our story tells us and others who we are, how we are, and how we move and express ourselves in this world. The construction of the story is unavoidable; it is a result of our parents, siblings, and everyone around us who contributes to our lives and interacts with us in interpersonal relationships. It is actually the story of our socialization, and it tends to stick with us. We internalize this story and integrate it into the understanding we have of ourselves and how we identify ourselves within the larger context of this world. Our story might resonate with us, but it could also feel unfamiliar. And as we grow up and begin to experience ourselves as individuals rather than as extensions of our parents, we start to question our stories. Eventually, we will 'free' ourselves from them (at least to some extent). How we liberate ourselves from the conditionings of our upbringing and become ourselves is one of the most important trials of our personal evolution and is a process that continues until the end of our days.

If we acknowledge that this movement towards radical freedom is a continuous process, we can allow some ease into the unease of it. You can rest in the knowledge that there is no magic spell to make you feel better. Our conditionings are in fact just imprints of other people's thoughts and lives: our parents, our ancestors, our colleagues, and so on. The commitment to engage in your own life as an ontological inquiry and to explore your life as an interaction with your surroundings and the people you are connected to will help to relieve your perspective. We realize we do not live within a vacuum when we understand that what we define as our reality and how we function in our surroundings is dependent on others too. There is a continuous interaction of ever-changing inter- and intrapersonal exchanges.

In a way you are always changing. Yet at the same time you are always the same. I'm going to invite you into a meditation to connect with the ever-changing and the everlasting within yourself simultaneously.

Mountain meditation

A visualization concentration exercise (15–30 minutes)

1. Find a comfortable seat. Settle in, supporting your legs and lower back. Close your eyes or rest your gaze softly on the floor in front of you.

2. Imagine you are standing in nature, at the foot of a mountain. It can be a mountain you know, maybe one you have actually climbed, or an imaginary mountain.

3. Visualize the surroundings: the temperature, the season, the smells, the sounds. Plants, trees, rocks, the colours of the rocks. Is there water or a stream?

4. Look at the very top of the mountain. What can you see there? Look closer. Then imagine yourself sitting at the very top of the mountain. Now imagine you are gazing out from the top and admiring the view. What can you see from where you are sitting? Other mountains? Water? The ocean? Trees? Woods and forests? Roads, houses? Look as thoroughly as you can, detecting colours, details, movements.

5. Then imagine being the mountain, and start sensing what is happening on you. The nature of plants, animals, winds, and weather. The sun or the moon, the season. What season is it? Imagine the warmth of a summery sun. The smell of flowers and trees.

Insects buzzing, animals moving about. Streams running joyously downwards. And as you gaze out at the landscape before you, begin to sense the slow transition to autumn. The greenest of colours become yellows, oranges, reds, and browns. Leaves begin falling. Animals feed on berries. Winds blow strongly, temperatures begin to cool. Rain falls. Frost. Snow. The landscape becomes white, the trees bare. Footprints appear in the snow. Winter storms arrive with hail and freezing cold. Night and day. Day and night. Sunrises. Sunsets. With the sunrise, heat rises. It becomes warmer. Snow begins to melt. Animals reappear. You hear water dripping, streams filling, water running fast and downwards to the lakes. Green colours sprout. Trees start to blossom. Flowers appear. Warm temperatures arrive, and nature bursts with abundance. This change of seasons happens again and again and again . . .

6. As you visualize and imagine the transitions of the seasons, remind yourself that it has been like this for aeons. The mountain has endured year after year, season after season, change after change. This is the ever-changing nature of the mountain. Centuries, thousands of years, hundreds of thousands of years have passed since the mountain formed, and this change has been continuous. Yet, at the same time, the mountain is always the same. Never changing, ever-changing.

7. And so are you. Ever-changing. Never changing. The essence of you is always there. And yet you are also always changing. You are an evolving, growing,

maturing, transitioning being. Just like every human being. Yet like no one else. Just like you.

8. Now start to return to yourself. Imagine again you are sitting on the very top of the mountain, gazing out at the view. Look all the way down to the very foot of the mountain where you began this journey.

9. Then place yourself down there again. Look up at the mountaintop where you were just seated, then take in the mountain in its wholeness. Take in the colours and structures.

10. Return to your body, here and now. Feel your breath moving in and out of you. Feel your breath moving in your body. Feel how your body connects to the ground.

11. And when you feel ready, gently open your eyes.

· ·

Integration

A practice of connecting the dots

When engaging in the above exercise, was there one thing (or more) you noticed?

- Regarding your breath?
  For example: the rhythm. The depth. Change of quality. The difference between inhale and exhale. Please describe.

- In your body or connected to bodily sensations?
  For example: a sensation being intensely present. Some discomfort or comfort. One small area asking for all your attention, or a larger area of the body. Different sensations, some subtle, others obvious. Prickling, tickling, or temperature changes. Please describe.

- Regarding the activity of your mind or the movement of thoughts?
  For example: thoughts moving fast or slowly. One idea, thought or situation demanding your attention. Or were there many thoughts present, maybe scattered or jittery. Did you notice a shift in focus or attention? Did your quality of mind become clearer or more foggy? Please describe.

- In your emotions?
  For example: did you notice any emotion(s)? Did you

notice any emotions rising and passing? Fading? Or perhaps you became aware of the intensity of emotions becoming stronger or lighter. Please describe.

You are not who you think you are

You are not what you think and you are not what you feel. Nor are you the sensations in your body. You are none of this, you are more than your parts. It is the combination of all these parts in a magical configuration that makes you *you*. In times of struggle we feel fragmented, and we can then feel like we are any of those parts separately. Our pain is maintained as we focus on just one or two parts, and the experience of being feels incomplete. It feels like this because our parts are not attuned. We feel at ease again when we feel whole, and we feel whole when the parts come together as in a symphony. They fold into each other in a meaningful way. When this happens, you can feel that you are more than the overwhelming negative thoughts, or more than the paralysing anxiousness. Or more than the uncomfortable sensations in the body. This feeling of being whole is what we move towards when we inquire into our inner dark, pausing and tolerating the everlasting ebb and flow.

If you experience a lack of harmony between who you feel you are and how you feel, this feeds the unease. If *who* you feel you are doesn't resonate with *how* you feel and *what* you do, the struggle will be experienced more intensely. And we can flip that thought: if you don't know how you feel, you won't know what you need to be doing to be happy and at ease. Your sense of self will be weak. One of my teachers offered a simple and beautiful practice for such moments, which I will share a little later in this chapter. It is called 'Hello, my love.'

It is true that everyone has moments in which they waver. In my psychotherapy practice and with my yoga students, among fellow dharma practitioners, and of course within myself, the same issues arise. From the priest in doubt, to the refugee with unfathomable experiences, to the yoga teacher, or the aggressive businessman, to the full-time mother, or the doctor – all are wounded by struggle and all feel a universal pain. We share this. But we must all walk through our own process and transform those wounds into wisdom in order to reconnect with our Inner Spark.

You and the narrating voice

From the moment we learn to talk, we start a conversation with ourselves. This inner dialogue is a tool in our set of self-regulating techniques. Children tend to speak out loud and share this self-conversation, often clearly narrating what they are doing as they do it. It is a form of play. They thicken the plot around what they are doing, adding what they are thinking, imagining, and feeling, and they share it for all near enough to hear. At a certain age they begin to internalize this self-regulating conversation and speak to themselves in silence. And that narrating voice in the head can often become two-faced (or multi-faced). The tone of voice used in this inner conversation is based on an intricate mix of our own personality traits, how we interact with our family members and/or our caregivers, and how we move about in our surroundings. The two-faced inner voice is heard in one voice talking you up, and in the other one talking you down. These two sides of yourself may not agree much. And the more uneasy and uncomfortable we feel, the more heated the debate between these two usually is. When things are rough and we start feeling down, one of these voices is taking a lead. You can guess which one.

There is much to be said for noticing your inner dialogue. And great benefits if you can notice what the two voices are saying. Can you try to hear what your inner critic is saying? If you can notice when it is loudly present within you, you will see which core beliefs about yourself it is trying to reinforce. And if you can hear all of this, maybe you can also notice whose voice it is you are hearing. Is it you, or have you copied this from someone else in your life?

You may have heard the following golden rules of communication before. But did you know they apply to both inner and outer dialogue? In times of struggle, you can use them to check in with yourself and evaluate what you are saying to yourself.

- Is it true? For whom is it true? How do you know it is true?

- Is it necessary to say it? What is the intention behind it? What do you wish to achieve by saying it?

- Is it the right time to say it? What are the possible consequences?

- Can you say it differently? How can you say it in a kinder and more loving way?

Who are you now?

To know who you are is a lifelong inquiry. And honestly, I cannot promise you'll ever arrive fully at this destination, as there are parts of us that will always be changing and will be unknown because of that. However, fortunately some parts are more or less consistent and can be known. For each phase of life, different things are important to us. But (as we saw in Part I) our feelings of belonging within our communities, and our social roles within them, will almost always determine how we feel about ourselves. These inform our sense of identity, our sense of self, and give our lives meaning and purpose. And yet this seems to be a vulnerable way for us to view ourselves. Don't we want to feel grounded and able to stand strongly in ourselves in times of emotional struggle, regardless of our social roles? Don't we want to feel strong regardless of what we do in our communities? This is challenging and can also be difficult to grasp as an idea since our society shapes us to blend in according to our social roles. Think about it for a moment: who are you right now? Try to unravel yourself, your sense of identity, from the social roles, titles, and accomplishments you use to define yourself. Think instead about who you are, as a human, in this world, at this moment. We'll return to this a bit later in the chapter.

Wisdom practices of yoga and mindfulness are a helpful way to get to know yourself better, in your own time, on your own terms. Each time you practise it is like peeling away the layers of an onion. When you engage in formal practice (seated or moving meditation), you connect with yourself deeply. And by deeply, I mean you allow an experience of being fully in your own body, spending time with yourself, teaching yourself to regulate the nervous system and bring it to at-ease mode (or at least as much as possible). In this space of presence, a sense of contact with yourself is more available to you. And over time, as you continue to practise, this connection allows for a better understanding of yourself. As you come to know the parts of yourself better you can hold them with kindness.

Our body is a resource that we can ground ourselves in when we get lost in ruminating thoughts or restless ambitions. Yet sometimes the body doesn't feel like a safe space and there might be too little connection. It is essential you befriend your body. Taking care of ourselves by being centred in our bodies is more efficient than leaving self-care to just thoughts and words. Knowing yourself through aware experience of being in your body gives a deeper wisdom than knowing yourself through thoughts alone. Your thoughts tend to speak more loudly than your body. And, as we've seen throughout this book, thoughts are not to be trusted blindly. However, understanding what's going on inside your body, interoception, can be trusted. And this experience can help us develop new strength and vocabulary regarding our emotions. And we can all benefit from a better understanding of our emotional realms.

There's a lot to say about our emotional bodies and how we express these parts of ourselves within the contexts of our culture. We talked about emotional competence earlier, and defined this as our ability to recognize emotions, but also how we tolerate them, how we embody them, and what we know about them – both in ourselves and others. Our functioning as beings on this planet depends on how we live in our societies, cities, and communities, and includes fellowship with our neighbours. Emotional competence is a crucial component to our functioning. A higher level of emotional competence means we can support ourselves, and each other, better – perhaps even with more equanimity.

We can view the body as a gateway towards more emotional competence. When we are able to dive confidently into the emotional realm as found in the body, we can remain grounded in our essence more easily, despite the emotional turmoil or struggle as it presents in thoughts. We can also access our sense of self, regardless of the social tags, roles, and functions we identify with. We have access to our values, and what we feel guided by, from a space of strength and truth. Our bodies speak to us with accuracy. But when the connection to ourselves through the body is poor, the information our body gives us may not be accurate at all. It's like our inner alarm system is not well calibrated and the communicative pathways in our brain are rusty. Body-based and meditative practices can help with this and help restore these connections. I'll give you an example.

For those of you who have practised yoga or meditation for a while, you may know that feeling after deep practice you sometimes get that is often referred to as a 'yoga high'. You experience a boost of feel-good hormones in the brain and body and a decrease in stressed-out hormones. The neurochemical flow associated with this feeling goes something like this, no matter what baseline you have: there is an increase in serotonin (the happy neurotransmitter), which reduces cortisol (stress) and anxiety hormones, which releases endorphins and melatonin, which stimulates the release of oxytocin (the love chemical), and balances dopamine (the reward chemical). This flow sets you up for a relaxed and happy inner experience of feeling safe, balanced, and at ease. When we feel like this, the emotional realm, or diving into the dark waters of our inner lakes, suddenly feels accessible. At this point the unravelling can begin. This is why many people feel emotional and find tears flowing after a yoga or meditation class, even if they are not aware of the reasons. You have simply prepared your inner landscape to access those feelings, safely and on your own terms.

Feel your feelings

An experience-based practice

In this exercise you are invited to grow your emotional competence by experiencing your feelings right now, in this moment.

1. **Confirm your own emotions by acknowledging their presence**: This can be done by engaging in various body-based movement practices founded in the breath (like yoga, or 'movement poetry', as I like to call it). These practices facilitate a connection with the emotional body, and help you to access your inner emotional landscape by stimulating body awareness (interoception) and the felt sense. These experience-based activities support your ability to recognize emotional expressions in your body.

2. **Expression**: Once you've connected with the emotional body, and emotions are recognized, you can start connecting the dots. This is where meaning is found and it is an essential step in the process of moving onwards. You can begin to recognize emotions and then start to name the variety of feelings dancing within you. Emotions are objective, feelings are subjective – they are functional for you. It's important to name these feelings, and to express them in a skilful manner that serves you and your wellbeing.

3. **Give them space**: Write down all feelings that move within you, jotting them down as keywords. Or alternatively you can say them out loud as they pass through your awareness. Joy. Sadness. Anger. Shame. And so on. Feel every feeling as it arises and passes. Continue for 5–10 minutes.

4. **Sit in silence**: Reconnect to your body. Feel your body connected to the ground, your yoga mat, pillow, or chair – whatever you are sitting on.

As you engage in this practice – the peeling of your emotional onion – you will be able to connect to your inner narrative. You will hear the voices of memories, experiences, told stories, and dreams expressed or unlived. It is important that you are able to tell your own story, because when you tell it – each time you tell it, again and again – you peel away at the layers of the onion. As you access the inner landscape of emotions through the body, through movement poetry, you find the words you need to describe how it feels to be in your body. This creates confidence and feels very different to looking for words to describe something you don't know.

I call yoga and similar practices 'movement poetry' because they are a way of accessing your heart without words. We can only access what is alive for us right now, what is here and now. Cultivating mindfulness is exactly that. And it is also the practice of gentleness, kindness, and curiosity towards what comes up in us in a given moment. It teaches us to meet the story of ourselves without judgement and helps us retell the story when we do judge. We give the heart space, we don't deny it or resist it. There is a beautiful Dzogchen practice that is widely shared by the teacher Lama Tsultrim Allione, known as 'Feeding your Demons'. In this practice the stories of hurt, pain, difficult feelings, and unease are given space. We are asked to bathe in the darkest waters we know. When we do this we see why the stories are presenting themselves and we discover what they want from us and how they can serve us.

Ronald Siegel, a renowned psychotherapist, mindfulness teacher and author, visited the Arctic Yoga Conference a few years ago and we were honoured to have him teach a mindfulness retreat out on a regional island. One thing he said particularly resonated and has stayed with me: 'Connecting with yourself in meditation is like instant psychotherapy.' Accessing our own inner landscapes really does allow for the same spontaneous insights that can be accessed through the work of psychotherapy. But in these practices, you are not dependent on a therapist, you are your own mirror. Richard Freeman. a seasoned yogi and contemporary philosopher, wrote beautifully about this in *The Mirror of Yoga: Awakening the Intelligence of Body and Mind.* The essence of these teachings is simple: how we relate to ourselves and to what is present in our inner landscape, in a given moment, is what it all boils down to.

The stories we tell ourselves have emotions attached to them of varying intensities. How we are able to tolerate the emotions connected to those stories and narratives is what matters in the end. When we sit in meditation, or move and breathe on our yoga mats, or when we take a moment in our day for a potent pause, we decide to spend quality time with ourselves. One of my teachers at Spirit Rock phrased it that we say to ourselves: 'Hello, my love. How are you today?' Every time you sit in practice or take a mindful break, it's like you are saying to yourself (out loud or silently): 'Hello, my love. What is alive for you right now?' When you recognize the emotions connected to your stories and acknowledge their strength, you will see the whole kaleidoscope of what is alive within you, seeing each part for what it is: emotions are emotions. Feelings are feelings. Thoughts are thoughts. Sensations are sensations.

The most important reminder while returning to your Inner Spark and freeing yourself from feeling stuck to be your own best friend. Respect yourself. Be kind. Be patient. Act lovingly. And listen.

Ask yourself this: what is alive in me right now? What is present? Which stories or memories? What are the emotions connected to them? And what is the strength of these emotions?

On parents and parenthood

We've talked a lot about how it is to be you and how that came about. Let's flip the perspective for a moment and talk about the viewpoint of the parents and the caregivers. We need our parents very much, until we don't need them any more. Parenting is a tough job when seen in this light. Parents give their all to their children. And then, when their children don't need them any more, and wander off into the world (as the parents hope and wish for them to do), the parents are left behind. And then, to make matters worse, the children look back at their parents and begin to free themselves from the belief systems and world views they so carefully provided them with. Harsh, I know.

One of my teachers, Lea, used to talk about making sacrifices. She said that when we sacrifice something, we actually make it sacred. I loved hearing that and it really resonated with me. Becoming a parent meant entering into an omnipresent ritual and making daily life sacred. Chögyam Trungpa expressed this idea beautifully in *The Myth of*

Freedom and the Way of Meditation. He writes: 'Looking at an ordinary situation with insight is like finding a jewel in the rubbish.' I think this could be said of many things, but for me this is definitely also about parenthood. If we can come to understand that our children are fantastic teachers for us, any ordinary situation becomes a jewel. Our children are the embodiment of mindfulness. They live in playfulness, expressing emotions almost without a filter, or at the very least without excuses or intellectualizing what they feel. They are brave in this way. They also mirror us and show us ourselves. Even as they identify as a part of us, our children (before real social conditioning takes full hold of them) live in the freedom we are looking for.

Yet, at some point, parents become annoying to children. We all remember feeling like our parents were in our way or were too curious about our stuff. We needed space and we started the process of freeing ourselves from them. We didn't need them any more for our identity and we were more concerned with finding ourselves, even if that was a struggle. We may even have started to notice how their way of seeing the world had been woven into our conditioning. We may have heard their voices in our inner voices at random unexpected moments! Some of us may have rebelled and become angry with our parents, blaming them and judging them. As I said, being a parent can be a thankless job. But this unravelling of the child–parent relationship is normal and it's healthy. You have to rebel against your parents to find your own story. You have to unravel the threads of their conditioning that are wrapped around your own and decide which are yours. What resonates with your values now? You may end up choosing the very same values as your parents, but that doesn't matter; the point is that you free yourself from their stories about who you are, and you find your own storyline of who you are in this world.

I love being a parent and I couldn't imagine wanting anything else. But it's challenging and it has phases of real hardship. While you are sitting here reading this, I want you to think about your relationship with your own parents or your caregivers. How have you transitioned from being a child to an adult within your relationship towards them? Or do you and your parents/caregivers still interact according to the parent–child dynamic that was in place when you were a small child? Ask yourself the following: who are my parents for me now?

Who are you now?

A writing practice

In this Nudge to Action you are invited to put your story on paper – both how you understand yourself right now, and how you understand yourself in retrospect. Your inner narrative is an interesting and efficient way to discover what attitude you have towards yourself now and to see how you let yourself take up space in this world. It might also help you see root patterns of your current unease and struggle.

Step 1: Connect

1. Find a comfortable seat somewhere where there are few distractions. Make sure your lower back, hips, and knees are supported.

2. You can close your eyes if you like or rest your gaze softly on the floor.

3. For the next 5–8 minutes, engage in contemplation by observing any phenomena of the mind, arising and passing in your awareness. Whether it is a memory, or a fantasy or worry about the future, an idea or isolated thought jumping around in the mind, simply observe what is present. Without analysing, figuring out, changing, or removing anything from your attention, just trust that you are doing this correctly.

Simply observe the free-associative mind in this given moment.

4. Your aim in this exercise is to simply notice whatever moves into the spotlight of your attention, and then watch as it disappears and something new asks for your attention. You don't need to focus on anything in particular. Simply sit and notice what is moving within you. Notice how this affects you as you sit there.

5. To come out of this, take three deep breaths, inhaling deeply and exhaling fully, before gently opening your eyes and returning to the room.

Step 2: Who are you now?

1. Take your notebook and pen. Try to answer the following in just a few short sentences.

2. Who are you?

3. What is your struggle?

4. What are you impacted by? Write out some memories. You can start the sentences like those below, or make up your own:

   - My childhood was . . . and I felt . . . most of the time.

   - The quality of my relationship with my parents/siblings/friends was . . .

   - A significant relationship for me was . . . because . . .

- An important turning point for me was . . . because . . .

5. What are some stories of turning points or insights you carry with you?

6. What are your hereditary or ancestral stories (that you know of)?

7. What are three words your loved ones would use to describe the qualities of your personality, or other qualities that describe you well?

8. Now, think about who you are in this moment without referring to any social roles, work-related skills, or professional titles you might carry or have acquired. Who are you? You could start your descriptions with the following:

   - I'm interested in . . .

   - I thrive when . . .

   - I adore . . .

   - I'm inspired when . . .

   - I need to pause when . . .

   - I love . . .

   - I find it challenging to . . .

   - I practice . . .

   - I want to learn . . .

Step 3: Logging out

1. Once again take a moment to sit in silence. Give yourself 5 minutes to log out of this writing exercise, before returning to your everyday activities.

2. You can close your eyes if you like. What are you noticing right now? How do you feel? After writing all this down, what is present? Just notice what is present right now in your thoughts, your feelings, in your body. Sit with yourself in silence for a moment.

3. To come back, take a few deeper breaths and return to the room, opening your eyes when you feel ready.

Make sure to read the *Wellbeing Prescription: Playfulness* in the final chapter of the book, where function, dosage, and precautions are elaborated.

CHAPTER 9

The Path to Your Inner Spark Wellbeing Prescriptions

I know that this fresh summer breeze has played on many cheeks before mine. I know that this view has been here forever. Everlasting. Ever-changing. I know that the moose walking through these woods with his family has walked here before. And I know his ancestors walked over the exact same pathways. I know that we too shall pass, just as the autumn leaves fall on the earth and return to what they once rose from.

So far, so good

In this final chapter you'll receive your Wellbeing Prescriptions, eight of them to be exact. These prescriptions are your non-medical medicine, practices to maintain emotional wellbeing and to nurture your Inner Spark. These prescriptions will help you find ease in times of unease.

Hopefully, while reading this book, you found useful and new insights and have gotten to know yourself a little better by practising the Nudges to Action. You can always return to these practices, either picking and choosing as they suit you or doing all of them again in order. Practice these as they feel most beneficial to you. We will summarize the Nudges to Action and what you've looked into later in this chapter.

Part I: Normalizing focused on establishing the framework of the society we live in and the norms we are ruled by. We looked at how the societies we move in impact us at the individual level, affecting our psyches and mental health. Chapter 1 showed us that struggling is a part of life and that we can do ourselves a favour by embracing this fact instead of resisting it. Chapter 2 spoke about contemporary spirituality and showed that wisdom teachings have much to offer with regard to mental health. Chapter 3 helped us understand the many layers of emotional struggle and unease, and taught us what Inner Spark is. The aim of Part I was to increase your awareness of which factors impacting your health you can control and which you cannot control. Simultaneously we examined the many layers of our experiences and the implications these have.

Part II: Clarifying focused on how wisdom practices such as yoga, mindfulness, and compassion support emotional tolerance, and also looked into what your current situation and struggle is. Chapter 4 talked about the neuropsychology of inner dark and Inner Spark. Chapter 5 shed light on the obstacles standing in the way of change and what you must overcome when moving towards Inner Spark and radical freedom. Chapter 6 gave you tools to understand your own readiness for change within your process of transformation. The aim of Part II was to increase your awareness of your situation, expose what is actually hindering you, and help you begin to step out of struggle.

Part III: Agency focused on the action points that move you towards your Inner Spark. Chapter 7 discussed eight aspects for more skilful means of living. Chapter 8 allowed you to connect fully to your own story and invited you to do so from the perspective of the observer. And now in Chapter 9 you'll receive eight prescriptions for wellbeing. The aim of this part of the book is to provide you with the tools you need to gain perspective and to help you step out of emotional struggle in times of unease.

Finding ease in unease

This book is about how to relate more skilfully to yourself and how to find ease in times of unease. We've looked into why this can be so challenging and have found understanding for the inner forces that move us and keep us stuck where we are. We've seen that we need to practise finding ease in unease and that this practice will widen our window of emotional tolerance. We can strengthen this skill like we would strengthen a muscle, and with that find access to more skilful responses and behaviours. With practice we find we are better equipped and can draw more easily on these tools in difficult times or times of transition.

I hope you have found space to practise while you have been reading and to engage with the Nudges to Action. Now is the time to integrate all that we have learned so far. This chapter gathers all the threads of your process, summarizing the steps you are taking out of your emotional struggle and towards your Inner Spark. I want to emphasize that what you have explored while reading this book and what you have come to understand in yourself through these Nudges to Action are not to be seen as the final answer to your quest. Remind yourself once again that you are ever-changing and yet ever the same. And so is this process. The Nudges to Action and the following Wellbeing Prescriptions are *nudges* to actions and *recommended* practices. They are not the whole solution. Take what you need and what feels meaningful, and leave the rest.

I hope you know now and will remember that your current experience of unease is composed of a collection of influences that you have agency over and some that you don't have any control over. You don't have control over much of the contextual and situational, and least of all over the genetic. I'd love for you to appreciate this, and relieve yourself of the belief that you need to change everything. Instead, you can focus on that which you do have agency over.

Finding ease in unease is challenging, but it becomes easier when we know what the unease is actually about. It also becomes easier when we see that it is not always *what* we do, but *how* we do things that affects how we feel. And it helps if we can accept that there will be times when we feel stuck in an emotional struggle, and know that we will not drown in that. We must see that the only way to stay afloat and to move forward is to step into those dark waters and swim. Because you can only know your ability to float and to swim if you're actually in the water. You need to come eye to eye with the struggle and difficulty.

All of the theories and models we've visited are grounded within the frameworks of humanistic theories, leaning mostly on salutogenesis and Buddhist psychology. The main message in these schools of thought is that nothing needs to change. Instead, see what you have. See with clarity what resources you have available to you. See that you can evolve. Draw on your resources as they are now to find your way towards a more sustainable life, towards more emotional wellbeing, and to Inner Spark.

The path to Inner Spark

The path to your Inner Spark, how to get there, is best seen as a series of strategies. The following Wellbeing Prescriptions, together with the Nudges to Action throughout this book, are strategies to keep in your toolbox for finding ease in unease.

By engaging in various questions throughout the book, you've embraced self-inquiry and courageously investigated:

- what is causing you unease and the feeling that you are stuck
- the underlying core beliefs obstructing change
- understanding what you need to step out of struggle

These are the Nudges to Action we worked through, in order:

Part I: Normalizing

- Wishing yourself well
- Connecting with yourself
- Feeling your breath

Part II: Clarifying

- Gain clarity: know what you *don't* want
- Gain clarity: knowing what you *do* want
- Core beliefs and erroneous thoughts

- Readiness for change

- Potent pauses

Part III: Agency

- Readiness for change

- Potent pauses

- Movement poetry

- Mountain meditation

- Feel your feelings

- Who are you now?

Wellbeing Prescriptions

The point of these prescriptions is to increase your overall psychological health and emotional wellbeing. These Wellbeing Prescriptions are green prescriptions for mental health. They are free of medication and are accessible to you whenever and wherever. Along with the Nudges to Action, the recommended practices have the potential to empower and strengthen your emotional wellbeing and thus your integrated health. The prescriptions are for you to engage with and implement in your daily life, and they should nurture and nourish your Inner Spark. They are not to be taken instead of medical treatment but are complementary to medical interventions and psychotherapy. As with any prescription, there may be side effects. Precautions and rationales for each Wellbeing Prescription will be described as they are presented.

The aim of these non-medical prescriptions is to facilitate:

- relating to yourself more skilfully and with more compassion

- more awareness regarding what holds you in this current state of being

- knowledge of which strategies are helpful in times of unease

- development of more skilful emotional tolerance

The Wellbeing Prescriptions will remind you that it is what you do and how you do this, and not who you are, that will help you find ease in unease and empower you to step out of emotional struggle.

These are the eight Wellbeing Prescriptions:

1. Kindness

2. Patience

3. Togetherness

4. Nature

5. Pausing

6. Perspective

7. Movement poetry

8. Playfulness

As a general note: it is normal to feel that engaging in these prescriptions is most challenging when you need them the most. Therefore, please use them as a prevention tool as well as during recovery, knowing that they will support you later in times of struggle.

Wellbeing Prescription 1
Kindness

Rationale

Our culture is infused with values of pious hardship, and kindness towards ourselves is far from the social norm we have grown up with and are used to. Eastern philosophies and wisdom practices such as yoga and Buddhism describe kindness in various ways. In most contemporary yoga classes, you'll hear about *ahimsa,* a Sanskrit word which translates as non-violence. In your yoga practice this means not pushing yourself in challenging asanas (postures), accepting yourself, your body, and your thoughts and emotions as they are in this moment. In mindfulness-based practices you'll hear about *metta,* a Pali word which translates as loving-kindness. In the same vein as *ahimsa, metta* also encourages us to wish for health, peace, and joy not only for loved ones and others but also for ourselves. Wishing this for ourselves is often the most difficult part of a *metta* practice.

The practice of kindness is now commonly included in our healthcare system protocols since mindfulness and compassion practices used in regular interventions have increasingly been proven effective. This is true not only for the patients in treatment but also for healthcare professionals. The schools of thinking these practices come from are infused with the idea that being good to others is the essence of being. Heartfulness, compassion, and love to all beings are fundamental to the Eastern belief systems, and these balance the perfectionistic ways of our Western society beautifully. These practices allow for a different inner voice on the strict, ambitious, results-oriented one we are used to. This gentler tone legitimizes a more generous, kind attitude.

Recommendation

Start being your own best friend. Meeting yourself with kindness is going to do you good. This kindness is health-promoting and it will create more understanding for and acceptance of your current state. Over time it might increase your feelings of appreciation and gratitude as you deliberately invite yourself to take stock and notice what resources you have accessible to yourself, instead of drowning yourself in what you don't have or what is scarce.

Dosage

Formal practices you could do are meditations of *metta* or loving-kindness, self-compassion, or visualizations of opening the heart. Informal practices such as using your skills and efforts to help others is a beautiful way to remind yourself of your strengths and abilities. Start with ten minutes twice a week. Gradually increase to daily practice over the next month.

Considerations and possible side effects

Practising kindness can be challenging, especially if your sense of self-worth is low or if you feel very negatively towards yourself. When unease is high, the inner critic and self-judgement are also high. In these situations, believing the message of kindness is difficult. That is OK. Make an agreement with yourself that you can practise this now, even if you cannot feel it or quite believe in it, and then take in the message at some point in the future when you feel more receptive to it. This is also the way of kindness. You set some boundaries and clarify for yourself what is and isn't possible for you right now. Practising kindness involves strengthening your goodwill muscles and positive feelings. The practice won't necessarily make you feel good immediately, but it will help you build a nurturing relationship with yourself so that, in turn, you can have a better relationship with others.

Wellbeing Prescription 2
Patience

Rationale

When we don't feel well and our health is weak, and especially when we have emotional difficulties to deal with, we tend to experience restlessness. This uneasy feeling takes hold of us deeply and very uncomfortably, and when it's there the only thing we want is to get rid of it. Inner restlessness can make you very impatient and creates resistance towards what is happening in your inner landscapes. This resistance in turn makes you feel even more unease, more restlessness, and more impatience.

Practising patience can therefore be very helpful when taking steps towards getting better. The classical yoga text of Patanjali's Sutras calls for patience as an integral part of the practice process. It encourages returning to patience continuously, with devotion even, as a way to calm the ruminating mind and to find radical freedom from our conditionings. Through the practice of patience, we build tolerance and help ourselves overcome difficulty instead of becoming overwhelmed by whatever situation we are facing. As we practise patience, we learn to rest in the knowledge that difficulty comes and goes, and that whatever the intensity of our unease may be, it will not last forever. You can believe and hold hope that your symptoms are not going to last forever.

Recommendation

In the process of stepping out of emotional struggle, remind yourself every day to be patient. This will help you create space for kindness and bring more gentleness and softness into how you relate to yourself. When practising kindness, if you start feeling restless and impatient (you may feel you are ready for change and it's taking too long), remind yourself that this process takes time. Remind yourself how many years it took you to integrate your regular 'unhealthy' pattern of thinking or behaving into your life, then allow yourself time to unravel that and learn new, more skilful ways of being and relating to yourself. Be patient with becoming patient!

Dosage

Start by making a written agreement with yourself. Put this somewhere visible so that it reminds you of your intentions frequently and easily. You could even create a schedule for yourself, and plan check-in moments to evaluate your progress. Remember the kindness!

Another option is to put these intentions into affirmations and say them out loud to yourself. You could also write them out and then read them to yourself. You could say something like: 'I commit to being patient. I commit to this process of stepping out of emotional struggle one step at a time. I commit to encouraging myself to find and develop more skilful ways of being and to celebrating moments of gentleness.'

Start with five minutes every day throughout the first month. Then gradually decrease to weekly reminders. If unease is high, use these reminders every day.

Considerations and possible side effects

You'll be challenged, so know that this process will be difficult. In the beginning it may feel challenging every day. The feelings of inner restlessness and impatience can be intense. Remember that to overcome this, you only need to tolerate a little. Just take it step by step, hour by hour, day by day. You don't need to focus on everything that you want to change. Focus on the micro-steps and allow yourself to master these, one by one. Appreciate each moment of gentleness and try not to get dragged down when you feel impatient. It's all good. Just keep at it and remind yourself to be patient. Commit to the process, not the outcome. And most of all commit to yourself in the long term.

Wellbeing Prescription 3
Togetherness

Rationale

We human beings are group-oriented. We thrive in herds. Finding your squad, your crew, or your gang is therefore more important than you might think. Who we feel connected to and where we belong can change throughout our lives, but there are always a few people who mean more to us than others. Even for those of us who enjoy our alone time and can be alone without feeling lonely, our relationships are important. Togetherness is about understanding that investing in relationships is a matter of emotional wellbeing and is worth putting effort into. If you feel left out or like you don't belong, then ask yourself what you do to nurture the relationships you have. How do you engage with others? How do you nourish the relationships in your life? Feeling like you belong, and feeling togetherness, requires reciprocity. If your core belief is telling you that you don't belong, then find a place where you do belong. Where you do feel a sense of community? Start with one relationship.

Recommendation

Despite the business of our day-to-day lives, it is of utmost importance that we invest in togetherness. This is something we should consider when unease starts creeping up on us; when you feel discomfort it might be a good time to think about the relationships you have. What do your relationships mean to you? How are they meaningful? Who do you consider closest to you? Who feels less close? Spend time with people. Be social. Engage in their lives. Care about someone. Invite someone over for a cup of tea and a chat. Show interest in them, and they will show interest in you.

Dosage

Make sure to set aside time for weekly meetings in times of struggle. At least once a week, and more if you can. If it is too much for you to go out for a cup of tea, then invite someone over. Call your family. Connect with friends. Reach out and spend time with others.

Considerations and possible side effects

It is obvious that this can be tricky, especially if you are ruled by core beliefs that you don't fit in or if you feel stuck in loneliness. For this prescription, both kindness and patience are useful strategies to lean on. If you feel awkward or insecure in social settings, fully engaging in relationships or forming new ones can be very challenging. If this is the case, then try lowering the bar. Take one small step instead of letting yourself become overwhelmed by setting high expectations. For instance, instead of fixing the difficult relationship you've had with your father all your life, you could start by having one short conversation. Or if the only thing you want is to find a partner and get married, you could start by having a cup of coffee with your colleague. Invest in others, and they will invest in you.

Wellbeing Prescription 4
Nature

Rationale

Nature is good for us. The sensory input that we receive in natural environments is less intense than in cities, and being near natural elements – water, earth, plants, air – affects our state of mind positively. Biophilic theory and attention-restoration theory both show that we thrive, function best, and are generally happier when we are connected to and interacting with nature. Sensing the weather, taking in the views, and being close to other living beings has been proven to have a positive impact on our mental health. Research shows nature has positive effects on mental fatigue, stress-related conditions, and focus and attention issues, as it increases a sense of ease and inner peace and helps with concentration. In addition to the advantages of simply getting some fresh air and moving the body when we are in nature, there appear to be multiple other benefits to heading outdoors, and exposure to nature can be seen as a restorative and health-promoting activity. It's also free and sustainable.

Recommendation

Take a walk on the beach or in fields. Go to the park. Hike in the mountains or swim outdoors. Watch birds fly among the trees, or gaze out towards the horizon from panoramic viewpoints. Observe ants as they busy themselves, or take care of your own garden. Look at the trees and the leaves blowing in the wind. Gaze at the sky. Exposure to nature creates an experience of peace and calm. Interestingly, it is not only physically being in nature that has this effect, but also looking at pictures or listening to nature sounds that have a positive impact on our health.

Dosage

Engage with nature for a minimum of 15–30 minutes daily. This can include direct contact, or more conceptual or auditory interaction (e.g. birdsong). The likelihood of overdose is very limited. Nature can be enjoyed in togetherness. I recommend an increase in the dosage when you feel overwhelmed, sense mental unease, or experience emotional bewilderment.

Considerations and possible side effects

Being in nature doesn't cause many side effects. If you have allergies, remember to bring your antihistamines. Be sure to be prepared for the climate, and wear appropriate clothing. Don't go on extreme outings unprepared or alone. Respect natures' forces, and interact with gentleness.

Wellbeing Prescription 5
Pausing

Rationale

A potent pause is when you intentionally take time out from your daily routine. You do something to give yourself a sense of ease, and in doing so you stimulate parasympathetic activation of the nervous system. You literally press the body's 'pause' button. Potent pauses are essential for those who want to lead good and balanced lives. Pausing intentionally and choosing slow living means choosing a good life for ourselves. This is especially valuable in these modern times when we are constantly on the go, rushing from one thing to the next, and feeling stressed out about most things in our lives. We know that stimulating the relaxation response is beneficial and it promotes mental health and emotional wellbeing. Pausing is when you let your mind consolidate, take in and digest impressions, considerations, experiences. In this space creativity can come to us, and we give space to the unknown. For this pausing Wellbeing Prescription, I'd like to suggest you look into breathing exercises as seen in various yogic pranayama techniques, or breathing exercises that stimulate vagus-nerve toning. Many studies confirm the positive effects of intentional deep breathing. The nervous system can be seen to respond after just a few minutes of practice, especially when there is an emphasis on prolonged exhales.

Recommendation

Pauses can be anything that invite you to step out of the reactive mind or your autopilot mode. You can focus on informal practices like lying in a hammock, taking a walk, listening to music, dancing, or cooking – any activity that you can enjoy with some mindfulness and attentiveness. Choose an activity – off the mat – that invites you into a space of ease without ambition. Then add and include one formal practice here: choose any structural breath-work practice, as these are very efficient in hitting the body's pause button. Look for breathing practices working with prolonged exhales.

Dosage

This prescription recommends 30 minutes daily in which you take time for a potent pause. The aim is to invite some restful mental space into yourself by allowing contemplation without becoming caught up in ruminating thoughts. Allow yourself some midday rest or do some end-of-the-day journaling (spontaneous writing). Or go for a short walk in the morning and evening. For breath work, commit to 10–15 minutes in the morning and in the evening.

Considerations and possible side effects

When pausing in times of struggle, you will surely connect with your inner unease. This can trigger resistance and possibly behaviour that is not beneficial to your healing.

When unease grows and intensifies it can express itself as disease and disorder. The function of your symptoms might be to distract you from feeling the pain or the difficult emotions. In such cases, pausing could trigger more discomfort and pain rather than being helpful, and it would be wise to pause with sensitivity and find guidance on how to do this. For this reason, if your unease is so high that it affects your daily functioning and expresses itself as disease or disorder, then practise pausing with help or as part of a more structural intervention or treatment plan. The golden rule to keep in mind is that the more intense the symptoms are, the less tolerance there is for pausing. This is true especially when you are alone. If the intensity of unease is high then it is better to pause in togetherness.

Wellbeing Prescription 6
Perspective

Rationale

Having perspective refers to how you think about something, someone, or yourself. It includes skilful mindfulness, skilful concentration, and skilful understanding – and the whole process of working your way out of the narrow-minded tunnel-vision state that comes with struggle. You can stimulate yourself into finding new perspectives in a variety of ways – you can do this alone, in silence, or together through conversation. Finding perspective requires taking time to inquire into yourself and how you relate to this world. This is not done in a ruminating, negative way, but with an attitude of curiosity and with the desire to expand your perspective. The inquiry includes the wish to learn. You want to widen your perspective, zooming out rather than zooming in on yourself. Contemplation is a beautiful way to consolidate information and emotions into our systems. We cannot think our way through each struggle we encounter as embodied beings, and contemplation lets us step back very deliberately and explore the experience of being, if just for a moment. Don't expect your mind to be still. Don't try to stop your thoughts either. You can expect insights to drip into you, like drops of honey. You will come to understand yourself a little better and know yourself within this world a little better.

Recommendation

Some obvious ways to gain perspective can be found in various forms of psychotherapy. Another option is learning to find perspective through formal practices (on the yoga mat) like meditation. Any activity that sheds new light on your situation or way of thinking is recommended.

Dosage

In times of struggle it will do you good to engage in activities and interactions that move your perspective out of the tunnel vision you are caught up in. In the beginning, a couple of times a week will support you well. As the intensity of the struggle subsides, you can engage in these activities less frequently if they are therapeutic, or more frequently if they are meditative.

Considerations and possible side effects

Engaging in independent, non-guided meditations is not recommended when you are caught up in a severe bout of depression or if there is very high symptom pressure for other reasons. In such cases, being left alone with the negative chatter of the mind is not beneficial. Since meditations rarely alleviate symptoms in these cases, other ways to gain perspective are preferred. More active and interactive forms are better; talking to someone is always a good idea, especially if negative thinking has you caught in a downward spiral.

Wellbeing Prescription 7
Movement poetry

Rationale

Movement poetry can be many things. Find a gentle practice that coordinates the movement of the breath and the body. There should be a flowing quality to the movement of the joints, the strengthening and lengthening of the muscles, and an expansion of the connective tissue – combined with a mindful flowing of the breath. Mindful yoga practice contains all of these elements and is recommended. Over the last decade the body of research on yoga has exploded, and yoga is now commonly known to be beneficial not only for our physical health but also our mental health. Yoga can help us, over time, with positive lifestyle changes that will increase our overall health and wellbeing. The immediate short-term effects which are induced by deep breathing (so-called yogic breathing) include helping to tone the nervous system and temporarily pausing overreactive and unhelpful stimulation of the sympathetic nervous system. Many conditions associated with an increased stimulation can benefit from movement poetry, and it can feel more accessible than simply sitting in meditation or practising breathing exercises. With time, yoga can strengthen self-regulation, improve concentration, and increase meta perspective – the observation of the mind or thoughts. According to researcher and writer Bessel van der Kolk, a significant discovery is that trauma-sensitive yoga allows practitioners to regain a sense of agency over their bodies. Experience-based, bottom-up practices like mindful yoga give survivors of trauma a feeling of ease. Long-term effects impact neuroplasticity of the brain for lasting change, while immediately after the practice the chemical flow in the brain is already affected. This brings practitioners a feeling of ease, joy, happiness, or simply feeling softer towards themselves and more emotional.

Recommendation

Any movement practice that invites you into gentle flows and increases body awareness through strengthening the felt sense of the body can have a positive impact on your emotional wellbeing. Slow-flowing movement activities such as dancing or tai chi work well. Alternatively, you could try gentle yoga practices such as mindful yoga or yoga therapy.

Dosage

Practise any movement poetry of your choice daily. Take 15–30 minutes a day for this, especially in times of unease when you'll probably want to shy away from it. Go to a class anyway, book an individual session, seek out a yoga therapist or another type of movement therapy.

Considerations and possible side effects

Consider possible precautions. Despite the many health bene-fits, it is not always helpful to practise yoga. It's important to know what style of yoga or which practices can be beneficial in what circumstances or for what conditions. We know that practising yoga will alleviate depressive symptoms immediately after the practice due to the chemical changes in the brain. However, many slower, more silent practices – such as yin, with lots of silent pauses – can be too confronting if you are suffering from high symptom pressure or are deeply depressed. In such cases, dynamic flows are recommended over slower practices. Likewise, if you suffer from eating disorders and body-image struggles, then practising yoga in a studio with large mirrors is not advisable. A more gentle and therapeutic approach will be more beneficial to you if this is your situation. In choosing a yoga practice in times of unease, make sure you find a teacher with a sound knowledge of the practice as well as its therapeutic implications for mental and emotional health.

Wellbeing Prescription 8
Playfulness

Rationale

According to psychologist René Proyer: 'Playfulness is an individual differences variable that allows people to frame or reframe everyday situations in a way such that they experience them as entertaining, and/or intellectually stimulating, and/or personally interesting.' Studies show that playfulness supports multiple aspects of wellbeing and that it impacts overall satisfaction in life. In addition, there's a correlation between playfulness and health. Playfulness as a trait is closely related to extroversion and emotional stability, and it's been shown to be positively related to the ability to cope with difficult circumstances. Playfulness also gives us perspective. Research also shows that creativity is an efficient tool. A 2016 study by Tamlin Conner et al. explores the connection between creativity and emotional functioning, and establishes that engaging in a creative activity with playfulness daily will strengthen your emotional wellbeing. This upward spiral of positivity is highly promising and shows that we can take agency in building our own emotional health over time. Another study took on this question and found that engaging in creative activities decreases anxiety and the fear of death (Perach & Wisman, 2016). Let this research encourage you towards bringing more playfulness consistently into your life, especially during challenging times.

Recommendation

This prescription recommends time for playfulness regularly. Choose an activity you enjoy or love, like listening to music, dancing, climbing, cooking with friends, or anything creative that lights your spark. Children have a way of being playful through their physical bodies, actively exploring and inter- acting with their surroundings while simultaneously enjoying themselves fully. This is definitely health-promoting and you could let it inspire you. This is embodied mindfulness.

Dosage

In the beginning, make time for playfulness at least once or twice a week. Gradually work towards bringing playfulness into your everyday life. Ten minutes might be enough. The most important part is the consistency and frequency, so learn to keep inviting moments of playfulness into your daily activities.

Considerations and possible side effects

When you are going through a difficult time, especially if you feel low on energy, stressed out or sad, it is going to be harder to engage in playfulness or creative activities. In times of unease, we can get caught in a downward spiral that makes it difficult to find the energy for the activities that would best serve and help us. For this reason, it helps to plan for playfulness together with someone. This can motivate you and help you liberate yourself from the downward spiral. You need to put playfulness on your agenda, though, and you need to take action to make it happen if you want to see the change.

Afterword

The idea for this book has been ripening for years – from when I started jotting down passages, to when I began writing it from its start through to its end. From the introduction, and chapter by chapter, until this afterword. It was a book that needed to be written, as a dear friend once told me: 'What you write comes to you, and you can do nothing else than write it. When the words are on the page, they are alive in their own right.' I have appreciated the process of writing this book to explore and convey how the path of practice to Inner Spark relates to mental health and emotional wellbeing.

Nature is a beautiful metaphor for our inner experience. I grew up in nature, and its immediate presence impacted me in many ways. Its serenity, even in crazy storms, that sense of ease in unease. It allowed for contemplation and spontaneous moments of complete absorption. The coming and going. The intensity of cold, darkness, light, and warmth. The nature around us as a metaphor for the nature we embody is powerful. Our innate nature, of serenity, of ease and Inner Spark, but also the harshness, strength, and continuous evolvement. We are nature.

One thing we know for sure with nature is that it keeps changing from season to season. And we adapt. One thing we know for sure with our life is that there will always be change – transitions or life events, challenges coming and going, joyful moments. Change is inevitable. How we relate to it and to ourselves in the process carries possibility for growth. We need to be able to tolerate struggles, and we need to be able to find ease in unease. Moving through inner dark to Inner Spark, and learning how to step out of emotional struggle, allows for the possibility that that there is always ease even in times of unease.

As I look out on the mountains here from the hill where our house is, I remember how my grandmother and I used to talk about what it must be like to live up here with this amazing view. Their house was located at the bottom of this hill, and we could look right up here. She told me once that she knew a couple who owned a house up here. The house I'm now sitting in, where we are living, is that exact house. It's funny how this life goes. My grandmother told me, not too long before she passed, that she did believe in psychology. She had heard someone talking on the radio, and apparently it had resonated with her. And so it is. From mental health and psychology being some kind of ambiguous science, with lots of stigma around mental ill health, to moving in the direction of being on the curriculum of children as they enter elementary school. The formal practices of yoga and meditation, conveying mindfulness and compassion, bridge psychology to everyday life not only with more under-standing and embodiment through experience, but also with concrete tools to apply and find ease in unease.

I hope this book has been informative and useful for you. And I hope you found moments to practise and reflect. And most of all, I hope you see yourself with different eyes, with more compassion and gentleness.

And with this, I'll leave you the following little practice of meeting yourself with gentleness. Please use it as much as you want, whenever you need, to reconnect with your Inner Spark.

Meeting yourself with gentleness
Meditation

This is it. This is the meditation you need to evolve your relationship to yourself. To develop a kinder, more gentle relationship to yourself in challenging times.

1. **Take a seat**: Find a comfortable seat. Somewhere you can sit undisturbed, even if only for a few minutes. Close your eyes if you like, or simply rest your gaze softly on the floor. Take some deep breaths.

2. **Connect with your body**: Bring your awareness to your body. Feel the body in contact with the ground or with what you are sitting on. Take notice for a moment of how it feels to sit here right now. Can you feel your whole body, from the bottom to the top, from the front to the back, from inside to outside?

3. **Noticing**: As you sit, can you notice what is alive within you right now? The quality of your mind? What type of thoughts or stories? What feelings are present, connected to these stories or thoughts? What do they feel like in your body? Recognize their presence. Allow it space.

4. **'Hello, my love'**: As you notice what is present, can you silently say to yourself and to everything arising and passing: 'Hello, my love. Is this how this feels right now? And this feels like this. And this feels

like that.' Accept and notice any bodily sensation, thought, or emotion arising and passing. Meet it and greet it as you surf the wave.

5. **Return**: After sitting for a while, return your attention to your body. Simply notice your body, sitting. Perhaps notice the whole body, from top to bottom, back to front, from the inside to the outside.

6. **Breathe**: Take a couple of deeper breaths, and open your eyes when you feel ready. Take a few moments before you move out of your sitting position and go on with your day.

References

Allione, Lama Tsultrim (2008). *Feeding Your Demons: Ancient Wisdom for Resolving Inner Conflict.* Hachette Book Group

Claxton, Guy (2016). *Intelligence in the Flesh: Why Your Mind Needs Your Body Much More Than It Thinks.* Yale University Press

Coleman, Daniel (2005). *Emotional Intelligence: Why It Can Matter More Than IQ.* Bantam

Conner, T. S., DeYoung, C. G., & Silvia, P. J. (2017). *Everyday creative activity as a path to flourishing.* Journal of Positive Psychology.

Csikszentmihalyi, Mihaly (2008). *Flow: The Psychology of Optimal Experience.* Harper Perennial Modern Classics

Cushman, Anne (2014). *Moving into Meditation: A 12-Week Mindfulness Program for Yoga Practitioners.* Shambhala

Dufourmantelle, Anne (2018). *Power of Gentleness: Meditations on the Risk of Living.* Fordham University Press

Esfahani Smith, Emily (2017). *The Power of Meaning: Finding Fulfillment in a World Obsessed with Happiness.* Broadway Books

Fabjanski and Brymer (2017). *Enhancing Health and Wellbeing through Immersion in Nature: A Conceptual*

Perspective Combining the Stoic and Buddhist Traditions.
Frontiers of Psychology

Gaarder, Jostein (1991). *Sophie's World.* Aschehoug
Publications

Gilham, Jane E. (2000). *The Science of Optimism and
Hope: Research Essays in Honor of Martin E.P. Seligman.*
Templeton Foundation Press

Kabat-Zinn, Jon (2006). *Coming to Our Senses: Healing
Ourselves and the World Through Mindfulness.* Hachette
Books

Kolk, Bessel van der (2015). *The Body Keeps the Score:
Brain, Mind, and Body in the Healing of Trauma.*
Penguin Books

Kornfield, Jack (2009). *The Wise Heart: A Guide to the
Universal. Teachings of Buddhist Psychology.* Bantam Books

Perach, R, Wisman A (2016). *Can Creativity Beat Death? A
Review and Evidence on the Existential Anxiety Buffering
Functions of Creative Achievement.* Journal of Creative
Behavior

Porges, Stephen (2011). *The Polyvagal Theory: Neuro-
physiological Foundations of Emotions, Attachment,
Communication, and Self-regulation.* W. W. Norton &
Company

Prochaska and DiClemente (1984). *The transtheoretical
approach: crossing traditional boundaries of therapy.*
Homewood, IL: Dow Jones-Irwin

Proyer , R. T. (2017). *A new structural model for the study
of adult playfulness: Assessment and exploration of an
understudied individual differences variable. Personality
and Individual Differences,* 108, 113-122.

Salzberg, Sharon (2017). *Real Love: The Art of Mindful
Connection.* Flatiron Books

Siegel, Daniel (2007). *The Mindful Brain: Reflection and Attunement in the Cultivation of Well-Being.* W. W. Norton & Company

Siegel, Ronald (2010). *The Mindfulness Solution: Everyday Practices for Everyday Problems.* The Guilford Press

Trungpa, Chögyam (2002). *The Myth of Freedom and the Way of Meditation.* Shambala

WHO, https://www.who.int/ (Accessed 2018)

Williams, Teasdale, Segal, Kabat-Zinn (2007). *The Mindful Way through Depression: Freeing Yourself from Chronic Unhappiness.* The Guilford Press

Yalom, Irwin D.' (1992). *When Nietzsche Wept.* Basic Books

Yang, Boen, Gerken, Li, Schorpp, Harris (2016). *Social relationships and physiological determinants of longevity across the human life span.* Journal PNAS